Islam and Salvation in Palestine
The Islamic Jihad Movement

by Meir Hatina

D1523317

The Moshe Dayan Center for Middle Eastern and African Studies seeks to contribute by research, documentation, and publication to the study and understanding of the modern history and current affairs of the Middle East and Africa. The Center is part of the School of History and the Lester and Sally Entin Faculty of Humanities at Tel Aviv University.

The Dayan Center Papers are monographs, collections of articles, and conference proceedings resulting from research done by the Center's fellows, associates, and guests. The series is a continuation of the Center's *Occasional Papers* series, published since 1970, and is edited by Ami Ayalon, a senior research associate at the Moshe Dayan Center.

The Dayan Center Papers are published by the Moshe Dayan Center and distributed worldwide by Syracuse University Press, 1600 Jamesville Avenue, Syracuse, NY 13244–5160; and in Israel by the Publications Department, the Moshe Dayan Center for Middle Eastern and African Studies, Tel Aviv University, Ramat Aviv 69978.

Islam and Salvation
in Palestine

The Islamic Jihad Movement

Meir Hatina

 The Moshe Dayan Center for
Middle Eastern and African Studies

Tel Aviv University

Copyright © 2001 Tel Aviv University

ISBN: 965-224-048-6

Cover design: Ruth Beth-Or
Production: Elena Lesnick

To Michael Winter,
a mentor, a friend

Contents

ABBREVIATIONS

DFLP   Democratic Front for the Liberation of Palestine
(al-Jabha al-Dimuqratiyya li-Tahrir Filastin)

Fatah   Palestinian National Liberation Movement
(Harakat al-Tahrir al-Watani al-Filastini)

Hamas   Islamic Resistance Movement
(Harakat al-Muqawama al-Islamiyya)

IDF   Israeli Defence Forces

PA   Palestinian Authority
(al-Sulta al-Filastiniyya)

PFLP   Popular Front for the Liberation of Palestine
(al-Jabha al-Sha'biyya li-Tahrir Filastin)

PLO   Palestinian Liberation Organization
(Munazzamat al-Tahrir al-Filastiniyya)

PNC   Palestinian National Council
(al-Majlis al-Watani al-Filastini)

UN   United Nations

UNC   United National Command [of the Uprising]
(al-Qiyada al-Wataniyya al-Muwahada)

Foreword

The name Islamic Jihad is etched in the public consciousness of Israelis and Palestinians as part of the memory of the original Intifada ("uprising," 1987–92). The Islamic Jihad was present at the birth of the Intifada; its founders will even say that it was they who cast the first stone at the Israeli occupation. The Intifada had many fathers, and the role of the Islamic Jihad in its prehistory will continue to be debated between factions and by scholars. However, there is no doubt as to the centrality of the movement in the Islamic awakening among the Palestinians. Even if it was and still is overshadowed by the much larger Hamas movement, the Islamic Jihad exerted a decisive influence on Palestinian Islam in its entirety. It was the Islamic Jihad that forced Hamas to take the initiative in the Intifada and translate thought into a political platform.

Underlying the Islamic Jihad's outlook is the premise that Muslims and Jews are eternal enemies and that the duty of the Muslims is to wage a holy war until all of Palestine is liberated. This perception is now on standby. But should the full realization of the Palestinian vision regarding a political settlement with Israel be deferred, it is not impossible that its supporters will gain renewed momentum and move to the offensive.

Meir Hatina, in this survey, has compiled a penetrating, thorough study on the Islamic Jihad in all its aspects: ideological, political, social and organizational. He bases his study on the rich literature of the movement, which opens a window on its black-and-white, two-dimensional world—a world of fervor and self-sacrifice, and of taut anticipation of a general Islamic revolution. Hatina's contribution lies in his ability to understand the movement in its own terms, yet still make its logic intelligible to us. The story of the Palestinian Islamic Jihad has not yet ended, but its written record has certainly begun with the publication of this important work.

Martin Kramer

Preface

Palestinian radical Islam acquired its definitive format in the wake of the
Intifada, which erupted in late 1987. More broadly, it is a product of the
religious resurgence in the Middle East which began in the early 1970s
and reached a high point with the Islamic Revolution in Iran in 1979. This
religious revival, although activist and dissident, essentially constitutes
a defensive cultural phenomenon originating in the traumatic encounter
with the West in modern times. Its strength, as Emmanuel Sivan has
pointed out, stems from a blend of political and cultural protest.[1] It con-
tinues to be fueled by an identity crisis prompted by unsuccessful attempts to foster economic development and military power.

The standard-bearers of religious revival in the Middle East are Islamic
movements, which constitute a challenge to existing regimes, whether by
a reformist approach, as that of the Muslim Brothers, or a revolutionary
one, as that of the militant groups. These movements, often discussed in
the literature under the heading of political Islam or Islamism, may be
defined as social groups that seek to preserve, change or create norms in
the name of an overall belief system. They are largely composed of educated, urban young people whose sense of alienation from the state has
led them to internalize Islam as a framework for protest and struggle for
change. The fact that they are self-educated in matters of belief may explain their aversion to clerical Islam, which in their view sanctifies docile
submission to governmental despotism. Additionally, their exposure to
modern education may explain their willingness to make use of the technological advances of the West, albeit as a means to advance the struggle
against its aberrant culture.

William Shepard places the Islamic movements on the right of the
Middle Eastern ideological spectrum, under the category of "Islamic
totalism," which views Islam not only as a moral belief but also as a guide
to daily human conduct. It not only describes the social order in cosmic
terms, but strives to shape it. A derivative of this view is the concept of
the organic unity between religion and state in Islam, which, in Donald
Smith's view, rests on three components: an integralist religious ideology, internal mechanisms for supervising social conduct, and a political
authority that protects the faith and applies its commands. In nurturing

the intimate relationship between Islam and politics, these movements seek to justify their own claim to power. In contrast to the Islamic modernism of Muhammad 'Abduh (1847–1905), the contemporary movements tend to sharpen rather than blur that which separates Islam from other cultures. They display fewer apologetics, whether in relation to the status of minorities under Islamic rule or the implementation of the *hudud* (Qur'anic punishments).[2]

Lying at the other, leftist axis of the Middle Eastern ideological spectrum is "modernity," which tends to place great emphasis on the adoption of Western institutions and values, but without distancing religion from the public domain, as radical secularism does. Viewed historically, such secularism remained the province of a minority, marginal in terms of the consensus in Middle East society.[3]

In adopting a comprehensive premise, the Islamic movements view Islam as the sole alternative to a status quo that perpetuates passivity and failure. Only Islam has the energy to bring about a political emancipation crowned by power and prestige. In this context, Islam is cloaked in an aura of salvation and messianism. The salvation narrative is nurtured by a rich historic reservoir of cries of distress and suffering side by side with voices of triumph. The distress prompts rage against a bitter reality, while the triumphs engender hope, and even determinism, regarding the attainment of a historic turning point in favor of Islam. The experience of both these elements is deeply entrenched in the Muslim collective consciousness, constituting, thereby, a political asset for the Islamic movements.[4]

Generally, these Islamic movements lack a clear political platform, and their ideas, relying on faith rather than on systematic, reasoned thought, tend to be simplistic. Their approach to the public is formulated within a framework of general moralistic principles, exuding authenticity and self-confidence in a world of accelerated social change and an intensified crisis of identity. They tend to prescribe an ideal, even monistic, society divested of class struggle, oppression, poverty or inequality. Three central motifs constitute the core of their argument: (1) Islam in the 21st century is in greater danger of annihilation than at any time in the past, stemming from an evil design by enemies from within and without. The list of enemies includes the "crusader" West, the communists, the atheists and the Jews; (2) A utopian yearning for the glorious past of Islam and a passionate desire to renew it as an ideological response to the perceived threat to the very existence of Islam; and (3) A commitment to social justice and equality.[5] This profile largely defines the identity of Palestinian political Islam as well.

With the emergence of the PLO in the early 1960s, Palestinian Islam appeared to have lost its political vitality, making way for an intensive effort to consolidate a secular perception of the Palestinian nation based on territorial and ethno-cultural distinctiveness. Islamic rituals and symbols were indeed incorporated into the national discourse, but only as a lever to enlist mass support for political aims.[6] This subordination of the religious idiom to the national cause was prevalent through the 1970s, despite the Islamic resurgence that swept the Middle East and despite the presence of the Muslim Brothers in the Gaza Strip and the West Bank (the "territories"). The nationalist bear hug gradually weakened during the 1980s, however, with the appearance of the Islamic Jihad and later Hamas. These two movements, which played a key role in the Intifada, positioned themselves as an alternative to the PLO and established Islam as a legitimate political force in the struggle against Israel.

The extant literature on Palestinian political Islam has dealt mainly with Hamas, the leading Islamic force in the territories. The limited research on the Palestinian Jihad has not provided a clear picture of the movement and its various factions.[7] The most cohesive and important of these factions, and the subject of the present work, was that established in the Gaza Strip by a group of Palestinian academics led by Fathi al-Shiqaqi (pronounced Shqaqi). Its uniqueness was threefold: historic—its role as harbinger of radical Islam in Palestinian politics; ideological—its positioning of Palestine as the focus of confrontation between the Muslims and their eternal enemies, the Jews; and political—loyalty, albeit as a Sunni movement, to revolutionary Iran, and preparedness to grant it the leadership of the Muslim world.

This work is an expanded English version of a book published in Hebrew in 1994; it draws on numerous primary sources gathered since then, which further illuminate the topic. It explores a wide range of aspects of the movement, including its emergence and world view, its ties with other political forces in the Palestinian and regional arenas, and its way of coping with the challenge of peace embodied in the Oslo Accords. A special emphasis is placed on the movement's world of images and symbols, as an important medium of indoctrination and recruitment.

Transliteration of Arabic names and terminology follows the accepted rules in academic publishing.

I am grateful to all those who were involved in the production of this study. Special thanks go to Dr. Martin Kramer, director of the Moshe Dayan Center for Middle Eastern and African Studies, whose wide expertise and constructive comments were extremely helpful in finalizing the manuscript; to Professor Asher Susser, Dr. Meir Litvak and Dr. Ofra Bengio of Tel Aviv University for their useful comments; to Professor Ami Ayalon, editor of the Dayan Center Papers, who contributed his time and experience to enhancing the text; to Judy Krausz, who skillfully prepared the English version; and to Amira Margalit for expediting the publication process. Others to whom special thanks are due are Lydia Gareh, Elena Lesnick and Haim Gal of the Dayan Center.

Meir Hatina

Introduction:
The Rise of Palestinian Radical Islam

Palestinian radical Islam attained ideological and organizational maturity in the late 1970s and early 1980s with the appearance of Palestinian Jihad groups and their integration into the armed struggle against Israel. Its historic foundations, however, were laid in the 1960s, especially with the defeat of Arab armies by Israel in 1967. This event constituted a turning point in the attitude of Islamic militants in the Middle East toward the Arab-Israeli conflict. In their thinking, the debacle attested to the failure of the pan-Arab strategy of Nasserism and the Ba'th, and exposed the real face of the despotic Arab regimes as servants of "Western-Zionist imperialism."

This revolutionary view shifted the focus of the struggle from the external arena (against foreigners and the Jewish entity) to internal politics (against the ruling elite), and argued that the road to Palestine passed through the liberation of the Muslim lands from their secular regimes. This entailed a deviation from the reformist approach of the Muslim Brothers, which held that the Islamic transformation of society should be entrenched by communal means (*da'wa*).[1] The radical Sunni shift in priorities was aptly expressed by 'Abd al-Salam Faraj, the chief ideologue of the Jihad movement in Egypt, which was responsible for President Sadat's assassination in 1981.

> There are some who say that the jihad effort should concentrate nowadays upon the liberation of Jerusalem. It is true that the liberation of the Holy Land is a legal precept binding upon every Muslim...but let us emphasize that the fight against the nearest enemy to you has precedence over the fight against the enemy farther away. All the more so as the former is not only corrupt but a lackey of imperialism as well....In all Muslim countries the enemy has the reins of power. The enemy is the present rulers. It is, hence, a most imperative obligation to fight these rulers. This Islamic jihad requires today the blood and sweat of each Muslim.[2]

The militant message was expressed ideologically in Islamic circles in the territories, albeit to a limited audience. Yet, while Islamic radicals in the Arab states essentially distanced themselves from the armed struggle against Israel and deferred it to the distant future, the emerging radical orientation in the territories emphasized the need for an immediate jihad for the liberation of Palestine.[3] This orientation, however, was not translated into any activist framework, and remained the province of only a few advocates. Among the earliest preachers of jihad against Israel was Shaykh As'ad Bayyud al-Tamimi of Hebron, who served as imam of the al-Aqsa Mosque and who was expelled to Jordan in 1967 for religious incitement and subversive activity. Another was Shaykh Ya'qub Qarsh, also expelled to Jordan on the same charges in 1979.[4]

The state of lethargy of radical Islam in the territories during the 1970s was linked to two important developments in the Palestinian arena then:

1. The coalescence of the Palestinian national movement, which adopted the armed struggle against Israel. The rise of the PLO in the inter-Arab and international spheres, and its development of a multi-faceted infrastructure in the territories, reinforced the national identity of the local population. These two processes allowed the PLO to project itself as the legitimate representative of the Palestinian people,[5] a status recognized as well by the religious establishment in the form of the Supreme Muslim Council (established in 1967). The Council's close ties with Islamic regimes and bodies throughout the world, and its role as provider of religious services to the population, endowed the PLO with both religious approval and an important channel for advancing its political aims.[6]

2. The growing influence of the Muslim Brothers in the territories. Previously, between 1948 and 1967, the Brothers were weak and kept a low profile. In the Gaza Strip the movement was under systematic repression by the Nasserist regime, while in the West Bank it was effectively monitored by the Jordanian authorities. Furthermore, the emergence, during the latter 1950s, of such new political organizations as Fatah and the Arab Nationalists (al-Qawmiyyun al-'Arab) served to weaken the attraction of the Brothers.[7] The 1967 war, however, constituted a watershed in the history of the Brothers in the territories.

The cutoff of territorial continuity with Jordan and Egypt, and the need to establish a separate infrastructure reliant on the local population, led the Brothers to focus their energy on the communal arena. The Israeli Civil Administration displayed a relatively tolerant attitude toward religious activity, in part in order to undermine the influence of the PLO. This, and growing financial support from Jordan and the Gulf states (led by Saudi Arabia), allowed the movement to intensify its activities, centered on mosques, charitable organizations, schools, student councils and trade unions. These civil bodies operated as social and cultural centers, but also as a powerful bases for political activity.

Three main bodies coordinated Brothers activities in the Gaza Strip and later constituted a springboard for Hamas: *al-Mujamma' al-Islami* (the Islamic Center), *al-Jam'iyya al-Islamiyya* (the Islamic Association) and the Islamic University. *Al-Mujamma'*, founded in 1973 and legalized in 1978, was based in the Jurat al-Shams Mosque in the Zaytun quarter of Gaza. Its spiritual leader was Shaykh Ahmad Yasin, assisted by Dr. Ibrahim al-Yazuri, a pharmacist by training. *Al-Jam'iyya*, founded in 1976, was based in the Shati refugee camp. It was headed at first by Shaykh Ahmad Isma'il Bahr and later by Shaykh Khalil Ibrahim al-Quqa. The Islamic University, established in 1978, served as an academic extension of Egypt's al-Azhar University, with Saudi and Jordanian funding. It offered generous scholarships and easy admission conditions, drawing many students from poor families.[8]

The communal activity was based on the Brothers' ideological outlook, which viewed the establishment of an Islamic state in Palestine by means of jihad against Israel as a long-term goal that required preparatory educational groundwork. This vision was reflected in a policy of restraint regarding anti-Israeli activity, while intensifying competition with the PLO, which was perceived as the main political rival in the struggle over the image of Palestinian society.[9] Hostility toward the secular nationalism of the PLO was aptly expressed by a Brothers leader in the Gaza Strip:

> The land, all the land, will be either heretic land or Islamic land. There is no place for Arab, Palestinian or Jewish land....The land is entirely for Allah, and there is no room for consecrating the land, as consecration is for Allah alone. Nationalism as a tie to the land does not appear except in the sector ruled by intellectual and ideological degeneration.[10]

19

Other Islamic groups, and especially the Islamic Liberation Party (*Hizb al-Tahrir al-Islami*), kept a low profile in local politics and on the issue of armed struggle against the occupation. The Liberation Party, established in 1952 by a group of 'ulama' under the leadership of Shaykh Taqi al-Din al-Nabhani (d. 1977), espoused views that had little relevance to current Palestinian circumstances and attracted only a small following. It was dedicated to the idea of the restoration of the caliphate, if necessary by violent means, under Nabhani's motif: "Where a caliph is present, there will you find the Islamic state as well." This pan-Islamic vision also dictated the party position on the issue of Palestine by arguing that Israel was already challenged by fighting organizations; what was required was the establishment of a large Islamic state to confront it, even if this involved a long process.[11]

From the late 1970s onward, a series of developments in the region and in the Palestinian arena paved the way for the rise of militant Islam in the territories and its exponent, Palestinian Islamic Jihad:

1. The failure of various initiatives—Pan-Arab, Palestinian and international—to end the Israeli occupation and to realize the national rights of the Palestinians.

2. The religious resurgence in the Middle East, which highlighted the universal nature of Islam and its deep roots in Muslim peoples. The Islamic Revolution in Iran (1979), the murder of Sadat by Muslim radicals in Egypt (1981), and the guerrilla attacks by the Shi'i militias in Lebanon against the Israeli and US armies (from 1983), all served as major sources of inspiration in spreading militant Islam in the region. Socially, the religious revival in the territories was reflected in a proliferation of mosques and charitable associations. Politically, it was manifested in the strengthening of Islamic blocs on academic campuses and in violent clashes with PLO factions, especially those of the left. At the same time, groups of activists began taking firm action against social behavior they perceived as offensive to Islam, attacking coffee shops, stores that sold alcoholic drinks and movie halls.[12]

3. Internal schism in the Arab world and within the PLO in the wake of the Lebanese war. The shift by the PLO leadership to a policy of controlled radicalism—non-acceptance of the occupation, but at the same time avoidance of a direct confrontation with Israel and aspirations for political settlement—evoked criticism by Palestinians.[13]

4. The passive stance of the Brothers on the issue of armed struggle against Israel, which elicited protest by its young members. In fact, many followers of the Islamic Jihad were disenchanted affiliates of *al-Mujamma'* and *al-Jam'iyya*, the Brothers' main stronghold in the Gaza Strip.

5. The expansion of secondary and higher education in the territories, alongside depressed economic conditions, especially in the Gaza Strip with its high proportion of refugee families, which fueled a climate of religious fervor among the educated youth.[14] In retrospect, an analysis of the ages, education and social origin of the 415 Hamas and Islamic Jihad leaders expelled to Lebanon in 1992 reveals that 86.5% were young (20–35), 32% were students, school teachers and professionals, and 53% were residents of refugee camps and villages.[15]

The Palestinian Islamic Jihad emerged in light of these trends. It was distinctive not only in calling for an immediate armed struggle against Israel but also in molding a new outlook that projected the Jewish presence in Palestine as a Western bridgehead in the heart of the Muslim world. It held that the liberation of Palestine by jihad constitutes the first step in restoring Islamic superiority. This perception is clearly reflected in the following quote taken from the Palestinian monthly *al-Sabil* ("The Way"), published in Oslo:

> One of the goals of Israel's existence is to serve as a base for the imperialist forces that seek to prevent an Islamic revival in the Arab and Muslim countries. This is so for two reasons: to keep these countries under foreign control and to prevent Islam from resuming its universal historical role....The Israeli occupation is closely related to the condition of inferiority, separation and distancing from Islam in the Muslim lands. Thus, the move toward the liberation of Palestine by Islamic means will damage not only Israel and its imperialist allies, but all the false forces that stir up hostility to the Islamic revival in the Arab-Muslim world.[16]

The Palestinian Islamic Jihad was not a single central body, but a conglomerate of factions. These were sometimes contentious, but they shared a common ideological ground, i.e., an emphasis on the liberation of Palestine through armed jihad. The most cohesive and important faction emerged in the Gaza Strip in the early 1980s, calling itself, upon the outbreak of the Intifada in 1987, the Islamic Jihad Movement in Palestine (hereafter, the Islamic Jihad).

Chapter One:
The Islamic Jihad—Historic Milestones

The historic roots of the Islamic Jihad go back to a group of students from the Gaza Strip, many of them members of the Brothers, who were enrolled in universities in Egypt in the 1970s. There they were influenced by the activity of militant Islamic groups such as al-Jihad and Shabab Muhammad (Muhammad's Youth), and the Islamic Associations (*al-Jama'at al-Islamiyya*) based in the campuses.[1] Upon their return to the Gaza Strip in the early 1980s, these students began to spread the revolutionary ideas they had absorbed in Egypt, with emphasis on Khomeini's ideology. The new movement became known by several names, including The Revolutionary Islamic Trend (*al-Tayyar al-Islami al-Thawri*), The Independents (*al-Mustaqilun*) and The Islamic Vanguard (*al-Tali'a al-Islamiyya*). It was founded by two of the returnees to Gaza: Dr. Fathi 'Abd al-'Aziz al-Shiqaqi, a physician from Rafah, and Shaykh 'Abd al-'Aziz 'Awda, a preacher from the Jibaliyya refugee camp.

Fathi al-Shiqaqi was born in 1951 in the Fara'a refugee camp to a large and poor family originating in the village of Zarnuqa, in the Ramla district. His mother died when he was 15. Like many of his generation, he was greatly influenced by the Nasserist experiment, which, by his own account, prevented him from adopting socialism. Gripped by a sense of void in the wake of the 1967 defeat, he quite naturally turned to Islam. The defeat was later described by Shiqaqi as "more difficult than the fall of Baghdad to the Tatars, Andulasia to the Spanish Christians, or Jerusalem to the Crusaders."[2] Another major influence was that of Sayyid Qutb (1900–66), the ideological forerunner of Sunni radicalism, who defined the line dividing Islam from modern *jahiliyya* (ignorance and darkness) and denounced Muslim rulers as heretics who usurped the power of Allah on earth. Qutb's book, *Ma'alim fi al-Tariq* (Signposts along the Road, 1966), was depicted by Shiqaqi as "one of the important works in modern Islamic literature."[3]

Shiqaqi, studying for a BA in sciences and mathematics at Bir Zeit University in Ramallah, took part in political conferences and made contact with Shaykh Ahmad Yasin, a prominent leader of the Brothers in the

Gaza Strip who was to become the founder of Hamas. Shiqaqi, however, felt himself in a hostile environment at Bir Zeit because of the dominance of leftist ideas. Upon obtaining his degree, he spent a period as a teacher in a school in East Jerusalem, then left for Egypt in 1974 to study medicine at Zaqaziq University.[4]

In Egypt he came into contact with a group of Palestinian students who had no cohesive ideological outlook or political experience and were studying in various fields: 'Abd al-'Aziz 'Awda (Shar'i law); Nafidh 'Azzam (medicine); Bashir Nafi' (exact sciences); Ramadan Shalah (commerce); and Sami al-'Aryan (computer studies). The environment of the academic melting pot, and shared living quarters in a neighborhood that was one of the radical Islamic strongholds of Egypt, provided the foundation for the rise of the Islamic Jihad. Ties were also formed with Palestinian students at the Universities of Cairo, 'Ayn Shams and Alexandria. Side by side with acquiring knowledge in Arab and Western literature, Shiqaqi and his friends delved into the works of modern Muslim thinkers such as Jamal al-Din al-Afghani, Hasan al-Banna, Sayyid Qutb, Muhammad Baqir al-Sadr, 'Ali Shari'ati and 'Izz al-Din al-Qassam.[5] According to one of the group members, Afghani had shown how Muslims could internalize modern sciences and still preserve their identity; Qutb had set out the preconditions for the coalescence of an Islamic movement; Shari'ati had provided a model of a just Muslim society; and Qassam had served as an example of how to translate abstract beliefs into deeds.[6]

During the course of their studies, Shiqaqi and his friends established ties with Egyptian students from the Islamic Associations and militant groups, sharing these young radicals' scathing criticism of the Brothers for their reformist orientation and their disdain of other groups in the Islamic spectrum. Against this background of disappointment with the Brothers and the impact of the 1979 Islamic Revolution in Iran, Shiqaqi wrote a book that year entitled *al-Khumayni, al-Hall al-Islami wal-Badil* ("Khomeini: The Islamic Solution and the Alternative"). Published by the pro-Iranian monthly *al-Mukhtar al-Islami*, the book depicted the Islamic Revolution as "a historically unique model of a humane revolution." In it, Shiqaqi praised Khomeini's approach to unifying the Islamic nation, both Sunnis and Shi'is, while granting the highest priority to the problem of Palestine.[7] The book's pro-Iranian orientation was to become the identity tag of the Islamic Jihad several years later.

Shortly after publication in Egypt, the book was banned and its author detained for four days, in line with the Egyptian government's iron-fisted policy of blocking the spread of the revolutionary message. Upon his release, Shiqaqi began writing for *al-Mukhtar al-Islami*, together with his colleague Bashir Nafi'. Most of their articles dealt with the Palestinian issue, although a few touched on other matters on the Islamic agenda. Shiqaqi also wrote several editorials for the monthly. He signed his articles with the pseudonym 'Izz al-Din Faris, while his co-author, Nafi', used the pseudonym Ahmad Sadiq. Their true identities were revealed only several years later, in 1986, when a writer for *al-Mukhtar al-Islami* wrote an open letter to Shiqaqi, then interned in an Israeli jail, praising his contribution to the journal and his steadfast stance against the occupation.[8]

Shiqaqi's and his colleagues' proximity to Egyptian militant circles contributed to the radicalization of their ideas, but also exposed them to repression and arrests by the authorities, especially in the wake of Sadat's assassination in 1981. Shiqaqi himself managed to evade arrest and left Egypt in November of that year. Later, he would depict Sadat's assassin, Khalid al-Istambuli, who was executed in 1982, as "a champion destined for immortality."[9] According to Muhammad Muru, a well-known Islamic publicist and an acquaintance of Shiqaqi's from their university days at Zaqaziq, Shiqaqi later admitted to him that involvement in the internal affairs of any Arab state only harmed the Palestinian jihad and detracted from the struggle against Israel.[10]

Back from Egypt, Shiqaqi spent a short period working as a physician at the Muttala' (Augusta Victoria) Hospital in East Jerusalem, and then returned to the Gaza Strip, where he opened his own clinic. Gradually, he attracted a group around him consisting largely of students and graduates from their shared Egyptian university period who had been expelled from Egypt for involvement in subversive activity. The most striking member of this group was Shaykh 'Abd al-Aziz 'Awda.

'Awda (b. 1950), like Shiqaqi, came from an uprooted Palestinian family that had migrated from the Beersheba region to the Jibaliyya refugee camp in the Gaza Strip. Leaving for Egypt to gain higher education in the early 1970s, he completed a bachelor's degree in Arabic language and Islamic studies at Dar al-'Ulum College in Cairo and a master's degree in Islamic law at the University of Zaqaziq. In 1975 he was expelled from Egypt for membership in a "radical Islamic society" and, together with his Egyptian wife, set out for the Gulf, where he worked as a teacher in the United Arab Emirates. 'Awda returned to the Gaza Strip in 1981 and began teaching at the Islamic University there, while also serving as imam and preacher in the Shaykh 'Izz al-Din al-Qassam Mosque in Bayt Lahiyya.

Besides Shiqaqi and 'Awda, the founders of the Islamic Jihad, cited above, included Sami al-'Aryan (b. 1958), Bashir Nafi' (b. 1952), Ramadan Shalah (b. 1958), Nafidh 'Azzam (b. 1958) and 'Abdallah al-Shami (b. 1954). Other activists were Muhammad al-Hindi, Sayyid Hasan Baraka, Sulayman 'Awda, Muhammad Jada Tufa, Ziyad Nakhla, Fa'iz Abu Mu'ammar and Khalid Diyab.[11] The distinctiveness of the group was reflected in two interrelated spheres—politico-ideological and social.

1. **The politico-ideological sphere.** The aspiration to establish an Islamic state throughout the Middle East founded on the Shari'a and on Islamic values underlay the ideological outlook of the Islamic Jihad. However, its view of Palestine as the center of the Arab-Muslim world and the necessity to liberate it by armed jihad imbued the group with a strong Palestinian identity. Its political discourse combined Islamic with national struggle. Thus, the opposition of the group to Israel was twofold: it perceived Israel as an alien entity in the heartland of Islam, and as an occupying state suppressing the Palestinian people.

The presentation of Islam as a faith of liberation (*diyanat taharur*) constituted a reaction against the passivity of Islamic circles on the issue of armed struggle over Palestine, but also against the secularization that had spread through the PLO ranks. According to Shiqaqi, it was the absence of Islam from Palestinian politics that provided the main impetus to the emergence of the Islamic Jihad:

> Those who carried the flag of Islam [the Brothers] did not fight for Palestine, and those who fought for Palestine [the PLO] removed Islam from their ideological framework. However, we, as young Muslim Palestinians, have discovered that Palestine is found at the heart of the Qur'an. Accordingly, we understood...that the way of the jihad in Palestine is the way of salvation for ourselves as individuals, as a group and as a nation.[12]

2. **The social sphere.** The establishment of the Islamic Jihad largely reflected the socio-demographic change that had occurred within the

religious leadership since 1967. The group's leadership consisted of educated younger men in their early thirties from low to middle class origins, whose radical ideology served as an identity framework and as a vehicle for protest against the existing order. Most held academic degrees in the natural sciences or the humanities. The educated Muslim was defined in the movement's publications as the conscience of society, "the first to oppose and the last to break."[13]

In addition to the dominant academic element, the leadership comprised former activists from Fatah and the Palestinian Liberation Army (several of whom were behind bars), who provided both operational experience and public prestige. The self-image of these Islamic Jihad leaders was of a generation of "consciousness and revival" (*jil al-wa'i walthawra*) that had sprung up in Egypt and Syria during the 1960s and 1970s and that had ended the distress in the Islamic movement since the death of its leader, Hasan al-Banna, in 1949. This new generation projected Islam not only as the sole solution capable of bringing about a prestigious Islamic revival, but also as an important instrument in the restructuring of governance founded on social justice and equality.

Their personal charisma, modern organizational experience and active involvement in society enabled the Islamic Jihad leaders to project themselves as an antithesis to the extant religious leadership, whose origins were in the Brothers and the Liberation Party but also in the religious establishment. The movement's spokesmen based their revolt against the veteran leadership on the religious injunction that every Muslim must rely on his mind to arrive at the truth, and not blindly sanctify the authority of the leader—the 'ulama' or other Islamic figures. Opinions, they pointed out, were closely linked to the historic circumstances in which they were formulated. Thus, what is true for one particular society or period was not necessarily suited to another. To illustrate, Bashir Nafi' cited Imam Muhammad al-Shafi'i (d. 820), who, after settling in Egypt toward the end of his life, altered his views on many questions of Islamic law that had engaged him earlier in the Hijaz and Iraq.[14]

The religious leadership in the territories, with the open encouragement of the Israeli occupation, had drained Islam of all political and social content and turned it into ritual worship, the Islamic Jihad pointed out. This left the arena open for the Westernized thinkers and politicians, who had no qualms about corrupting Islamic values. The conservative 'ulama', with their legal expertise and social prestige, played an important role in people's daily lives, Shiqaqi conceded, but they were unsuited to lead the believers. The exceptions were those activist 'ulama', such as 'Izz al-Din al-Qassam, who rebelled against both the British and the Jews in Palestine during the 1920s, or the Shi'i scholars who led the struggle against imperialism and fomented the Islamic Revolution in 1979. They alone showed the ability to lead and inspire. Shiqaqi quoted Khomeini in calling for the denunciation of the official 'ulama' who serve as "the propagandists of the despots," an act that may be defined as "a victory for Islam and the Muslims."[15]

This blend of political and social protest facilitated the absorption of the new revolutionary message by the Palestinians, especially by students and the educated. Furthermore, the absence of an effective Palestinian leadership, and the erosion of the status of Jordan as a moderating force in the West Bank, created a political vacuum that provided Islamic fervor with a channel for self-expression.

Three stages may be identified in the history of the Islamic Jihad: political indoctrination (1981–83), armed confrontation (1984–87), and the outbreak of the Intifada, followed by the shift of the movement's center to Lebanon and Syria (1988 onward). Viewed retrospectively, Shiqaqi observed, these were "preparatory stages" (*marahil tamhidiyya*) that in large measure paralleled Qassam's moves in the 1930s. Their declared goal was the mobilization of the Palestinians in order to determine the struggle with the Zionist entity by an armed jihad.[16]

Political Indoctrination (1981–83)

The Islamic Jihad devoted itself, during its formative period, to extensive cultural and political activity in order to spread its revolutionary message and recruit membership. Its means included mosque sermons, religious conferences, issuing publications, and political indoctrination in the Islamic University and in Israeli prisons. Two foci of activity, which served as channels for political dissent, stood out:

1. Several mosques in central locations in the Gaza Strip, and especially the al-Qassam Mosque in Bayt Lahiyya. These mosques, some of which provided medical and welfare aid to the needy, served as forums

for radical preaching and as centers for membership recruitment. One leader defined the mosque as not only a place of worship but also as "one of the fortified strongholds to which the nation flees whenever imperialism penetrates the motherland."[17] The role of the mosque in entrenching revolutionary messages was well reflected in the Friday sermons of 'Awda in the al-Qassam Mosque. In them he spoke of the close link between Islam, jihad and Palestine, emphasizing the need to cleave to the religious commands so as to bring succor to the ills of Muslim society, reward the believer in the next world, and rebuff "every attempt to cut off this nation from its authentic roots."[18]

2. The Islamic University. Substantial efforts by the Islamic Jihad were devoted to ideological guidance and the building of an infrastructure on campus. As control of the academic administration and the student council was in the hands of the Islamic Bloc (al-Kutla al-Islamiyya), identified with the Brothers in the Gaza Strip, the Islamic Jihad established a student association of its own, called the Islamic Society (al-Jama'a al-Islamiyya). In annual student council elections during 1982–86, the society attained 4%–7% of the vote, with the Islamic Bloc scoring 60%, and Fatah and the Palestinian left 22%. The Islamic Society was involved in political power struggles on campus, which sometimes became violent, and published periodicals dealing with Islamic and Palestinian issues. These included al-Haqiqa ("The Truth"), Sawt al-Mustadh'afin ("Voice of the Oppressed"), Sawt al-Jama'a al-Islamiyya ("Voice of the Islamic Society") and al-Bayan ("Manifesto").[19]

The Islamic Jihad also spread its message in West Bank cities and in East Jerusalem. Its religious fervor was conveyed by students from the Gaza Strip who visited the academic campuses of Hebron, Nablus and Ramallah. Small periodicals were also circulated, especially al-Nur ("The Light"), published clandestinely in East Jerusalem, for which Shiqaqi and Nafi' continued writing under pseudonyms; and al-Tali'a al-Islamiyya ("The Islamic Vanguard"), edited by Nafi', published in London and distributed in the territories clandestinely. The movement's main forum for disseminating its ideas, however, remained al-Mukhtar al-Islami, in no small measure because of Shiqaqi's close ties with its editorial board.[20]

Religious fervor had particular appeal in the poor quarters of the Gaza Strip, where a new, educated generation was emerging, old enough to have experienced the social distress of Israeli occupation yet too young to have commitments to a fixed ideology, family or career. Shared dis-content with sociopolitical realities prompted these young men to inter-nalize new messages calling for immediate action to put an end to the occupation and its destructive effects on Palestinian society. The move-ment lauded young Palestinians who placed the advancement of justice and social morality, above personal interest. By contrast, it argued, young Westerners fasten on scientific progress, which is applied to the realm of destruction rather than development (for example, nuclear weaponry) and whose products are not distributed justly in society.[21]

Recruitment of members took place mostly by word of mouth—on campus, in mosques, and at school, during major Islamic festivals such as the Ramadan fast or *al-Isra wal-Mi'raj* (marking the Prophet's night journey from Mecca to Jerusalem and his ascent to heaven). These and other Islamic festivals, offered opportunities both for recruitment and for fund-raising to subsidize the movement's activities.[22]

Side by side with its civic activity, the Islamic Jihad also conducted clandestine activity by setting up underground cells of four or five mem-bers each. Their task was to implement armed jihad against Israel when the time came.[23] Another aspect of the movement's clandestine work was the printing of leaflets urging Palestinians to intensify their struggle against the corruptive occupation. An incident at the al-Aqsa Mosque in April 1982, in which an Israeli soldier shot at Muslim worshippers, elic-ited leaflets signed by "Sons of the Qur'an Movement" (*Harakat Abna al-Qur'an*). A violent confrontation between Israeli soldiers and students at the Islamic College in Hebron in July 1983 evoked another leaflet signed by "The Movement of Islamic Struggle" (*Harakat al-Nidal al-Islami*), which criticized Arab regimes and the PLO for acquiescing in Israel's acts of slaughter.[24]

Having established an infrastructure in the Gaza Strip, the Islamic Jihad emphasized its political nature and its commitment to an idea rather than to an organization. Regulating Islamic activity was indeed impor-tant and it was viewed as a counterweight to the secularism represented by the more Westernized parties. But, the Islamic Jihad pointed out, this should not come at the expense of the movement's ideological objectives. In modern times, Islamic movements sanctified the framework, not the message. They failed to understand the element that distinguished the Western from the Islamic organization: the former represented an exclu-sive group or sector, with a specific ideological program, while the latter represented faith, which was the province of all. As Nafi' put it, "The organization is a tool that ratifies the goal. It is not an arena for demonstrating haughtiness and authority, but a zone for promoting responsibility and awareness."[25]

This approach was reflected in the names by which the Islamic Jihad referred to itself, some of which were cited above. In retrospect, organizational flexibility was one of the key elements in the movement's success in gaining strength and public support, which reached a peak on the eve of the Intifada. Since the Palestinian Jihad consisted of an amalgam of factions, it could claim credit for the showcase attacks, most of which were executed by other groups operating in the West Bank and maintaining close relations with Fatah (see below).

Countering accusations by the Brothers of intellectual shallowness in its focus on armed struggle, the Islamic Jihad argued that pluralism in responding to the challenges of the time is religiously sanctioned, and that respecting rather than denouncing the opinion of the other was the starting point of true unity. Indeed, it acknowledged, communal activity was welcome and contributed to the welfare of the nation. But following the Brothers' path would not have contributed a new dimension to the Islamic movement, and would have meant ignoring the need filled by the Islamic Jihad, which restored the organic unity between religion and politics, faith and power.[26]

Moreover, the political nature of the Islamic movement in modern times constituted a practical necessity in light of the loss of the caliphate. In a detailed discussion of the Islamic movement and its relationship to social action, the Islamic Jihad organ, *al-Tali'a al-Islamiyya*, held that the establishment of Islamic educational and charitable institutions led to excessive involvement in maintaining them and exposed the movement to pressures for ideological concessions by the heretical regimes. Besides, communal activity left the oppressor and the tyrant in place, perpetuating Islam as a purifying sentiment only, rather than a political force aimed at overturning the existing order. Two institutions that did merit investment, however, were the mosque and the media, both of which played an important role in the struggle against Westernization and in heightening public awareness of the revolutionary nature of Islam.[27]

The centrality of Palestine in the overall agenda of the Islamic revival necessitated the positioning of jihad as the highest priority. Rejecting the charge of elitism, the movement stressed that its members came from the lower strata. It recognized, however, that at the present stage its main efforts were devoted to building an efficient apparatus rather than a popular structure, which would only limit its ability to act effectively against the occupation.[28] Quoting Sayyid Qutb, Shiqaqi asserted that the need was for a tenacious Islamic pioneering force to set in motion the Islamic transformation of society. The key to such a transformation was resistance to the occupation. Reflecting this approach, an appellation favored by the Islamic Jihad before the outbreak of the Intifada was "the Islamic Vanguard."[29]

The opening move marking the Islamic Jihad's entry into armed confrontation was the murder of a yeshiva student in Hebron in August 1983. The exposure of the perpetrators' identity prompted a large wave of arrests in the ranks of the Islamic Jihad, including Shiqaqi, who was known as the ideological and political leader of the group. Some 25 other activists were arrested with him. At the same time, 'Awda was banned from entering the Islamic University, where he was a lecturer.[30] In 'Awda's view, the large-scale arrests in late 1983 were palpable evidence of the Islamic Jihad's laudable activity, and represented the revival of the jihad spirit among Palestinians:

> People began to feel that the loathsome charge incorporated by a few corrupted claimants that Islam had no role in the battlefield was a false charge, and that Islam was the conveyor of the outbreak of the revolution. We have acted to present Islam in this sense...and have made it clear that Islam stirs revolution and opposition and does not recognize peaceful coexistence with any form of oppressor or tyranny.[31]

Armed Confrontation (1984–87)

The shift to armed struggle against Israel did not diminish the Islamic Jihad's civil activity in the Gaza Strip. On the contrary, Shiqaqi and 'Awda stressed, the military and civic aspects were intertwined and provided additional credibility for Islamic Jihad's slogan: "The Palestinian problem is the central issue of the modern Islamic movements."[32] The movement thus positioned itself in the middle, between the Brothers, which were devoted to educational and communal activity; and the Liberation Party, which adopted a strategy of change from the top down by violent means, with no active intervention in local affairs, until the establishment of the caliphal state that would liberate Palestine.

In the event, the standard-bearers of jihad against Israel, who from 1984 on mounted a series of successful attacks on it, were the Jihad groups, with their clandestine military character, operating primarily in the West Bank. These groups may be classified in two categories:

1. Groups established at the initiative of two branches of Fatah: the "Western Zone Apparatus" in Jordan, which had conducted anti-Israel activities for years and was subordinate to Khalil al-Wazir (Abu Jihad) in Tunis; and "Force 17" in Lebanon, commanded by Abu Tayb. The largest and most important of these groups was the Islamic Jihad Squads (*Sarayat al-Jihad al-Islami*), commanded by two senior aides of Abu Jihad who returned to the religious fold, Bassam Sultan and Ghazi al-Husayni. Another key figure was Munir Shafiq, a former Christian Maoist who converted to Islam and headed the PLO Planning Center.[33]

2. Groups that emerged outside the Fatah framework but were granted military training and logistic support by it. The leadership cadre of these groups consisted mostly of former high-ranking activists in Fatah who had been imprisoned in Israel. During that time they had absorbed jihad ideals, which they integrated into their nationalist Palestinian outlook. According to one observer, the Israeli prisons were "schools for revolution and the study of its principles," in which new recruits to the Islamic Jihad maintained strict discipline and obedience to senior prisoners.[34]

The first to organize a radical group in an Israeli prison was Jabr 'Ammar of the Gaza Strip, who was caught by Israel in the early 1970s and sentenced to life imprisonment for military activity. 'Ammar was released in a prisoner exchange in 1983 and went to Egypt, but was expelled a year later for subversive activity against the government. Another prominent leader was Ahmad Muhanna of Khan Yunis, a former officer in the Palestine Liberation Army who became a Muslim radical while in prison. Muhanna's charismatic personality and dominant leadership in prison prompted the Israeli authorities to isolate him from the rest of the prisoners and later to expel him to Lebanon (December 1988).[35] In an interview in 1993, Muhanna admitted that he had maintained close ties with Shiqaqi's group, but that he had independently operated secret cells which carried out attacks in the Gaza Strip as early as 1978–79.[36]

The liaison between Fatah and the military Jihad groups in the West Bank was Hebron-born Shaykh As'ad Bayyud al-Tamimi (1924–97), who had been ordained as a religious scholar and qadi at al-Azhar University in Egypt in 1949. He began his political career in the Brothers, followed by membership in the Liberation Party in Jordan, but left them because their platform ignored the centrality of the Palestinian problem and deferred jihad against Israel to the distant future. Inciteful sermons delivered by Tamimi as imam of the al-Aqsa Mosque led to his expulsion by Israel in 1969. His views were set out in several essays, especially *Zawal Isra'il Hatmiyya Qur'aniyya* ("Israel's Extinction—A Qur'anic Inevitability," published in 1980). In this book, Tamimi cites proofs from the Qur'an of the importance of Palestine to Islam and to the struggle against the Jews. In his opinion, jihad in Palestine is meant not only to restore a sanctified land to the Muslims, but also to put an end to the presence of the Jews, who are disseminators of religious heresy. Tamimi's impressive religious persona and his close ties with the Fatah elite as well as with Iran's leaders evoked strong support for him among Islamic radicals in the territories. Preaching his revolutionary ideas and establishing an operational base of support in Jordan, Tamimi succeeded in imbuing the clandestine jihad groups with the ideological depth that had been lacking heretofore. Additionally, he operated a clandestine group of Islamic activists for Fatah called the Islamic Society (*al-Jama'a al-Islamiyya*), which carried out attacks in Jerusalem and Hebron.[37]

Fatah's massive support of the military Jihad groups reflected its desire to harness the religious fervor in the territories to advancing the Palestinian national struggle, as well as to prevent the rise of an independent competitor outside the PLO sphere of influence. A conducive factor was the positive attitude displayed by Fatah to Islam, stemming partly from the Islamic background of some of its leaders, who were former members of the Brothers and the Liberation Party during the early 1950s (e.g., 'Arafat, Abu Jihad, Abu Iyyad and Hani and Khalid al-Hasan). In contrast to the Palestinian left, which eschewed religion in the public domain, Fatah recognized the driving force of Islam in society and sought to blend it into its nationalist outlook.[38]

Parallel to placing the West Bank Jihad groups under its protection, Fatah carefully maintained ties with the Islamic Jihad, whose stronghold was in the Gaza Strip. Their shared emphasis on armed struggle against the occupation laid the foundation for an operative alliance, albeit limited and unofficial. This alliance served the needs of both sides: the Islamic Jihad needed Fatah's extensive infrastructure in order to entrench its presence, and Fatah sought to harness this revolutionary group in order to erode the influence of its rival, the Brothers. With this, the Islamic Jihad zealously guarded its independent identity, maintaining that Palestinian nationalism was alien to the spirit of Islam, for it relied on ethnic origin and a secular outlook, while Islam sanctified unity that relied on faith and a metaphysical outlook. According to the movement's organ, *al-Nur*, "It is impossible to maintain national unity between faith and heresy, between truth and falsehood, between divine justice and human oppression."[39] This approach dictated the movement's position of retaining only a loose operative tie with Fatah and its dependents, the Jihad groups in the West Bank.

The link between West Bank Jihad activists and their colleagues in the Gaza Strip was forged during time served in Israeli prisons. Jail time was utilized for joint "seminars" with the aim of molding the consciousness of the Muslim activist. With the release of the first prisoners in the major prisoner-of war-exchanges of May 1985, the groundwork was laid for the renewal of military activity in the Gaza Strip and the West Bank (especially in the Nablus-Jenin-Tul Karm triangle).[40]

Religious fervor was reflected in 1985–86 in a series of attacks on Israeli citizens as well as on local residents suspected of heresy against Islam or cooperating with Israel. All these prompted a speedy response from the military authorities. Shiqaqi, the political leader of the Islamic Jihad, was arrested in March 1986, convicted of smuggling arms into the Gaza Strip, and sentenced to four years imprisonment. At the same time, 'Awda, the spiritual leader of the movement, was released from prison after serving a term of eleven months for religious incitement. Although careful not to associate himself with subversive activity, he resumed his fervent weekly sermons at the al-Qassam Mosque.

Islamic zeal spread in the West Bank as well. Acts of sabotage and knifings carried out there by Jihad cells gained political support in the Palestinian street, reaching a climax with an attack on IDF soldiers in Jerusalem (October 1986). The perpetrators were three members of the Islamic Jihad Squads operating under Fatah guidance. The three admitted, under interrogation, that they had convened separately with 'Awda at his residence in the Gaza Strip before the attack. His role in the attack, however, was not clarified, although the incident lent further credence to the ties between the Islamic Jihad and other Jihad factions in the West Bank.[41]

Another wave of arrests of Jihad members in the Gaza Strip followed in the wake of this attack in December 1986. Forty-eight persons were held on suspicion of murdering Israelis and throwing hand grenades at IDF patrols. Two noted detainees, formerly activists in the Popular Front for the Liberation of Palestine (PFLP), were Misbah al-Suri and 'Abd al-Rahman Jamal al-Qiq. In addition, several buildings adjacent to the al-Qassam Mosque, which had provided welfare services, were closed.[42] Attempts by rival Palestinian elements to take credit for the Jihad attacks demonstrated that radical Islam had become a reality that could not be ignored. Clear evidence of this was provided by a chain of events in 1987.[43]

On 18 May 1987, six high-ranking Islamic Jihad activists imprisoned in the central jail in Gaza made a successful escape. Shiqaqi, who was also imprisoned there, was transferred to the prison in Ramla and interrogated at length. Despite a widespread police hunt, the group of escapees, led by Misbah al-Suri, carried out carefully planned attacks against Israeli targets. These attacks, such as the murder of an Israeli officer in Gaza in August 1987, enhanced the prestige of the Islamic Jihad, whose operational capability had been severely reduced by numerous arrests in its ranks. They also provided renewed momentum for sabotage efforts by the Jihad cells in the West Bank.[44]

The fugitive band was eliminated only in early October. Misbah al-Suri was shot by Israeli soldiers near al-Burayj refugee camp on 1 October. Three other members of the band were killed in the Shaja'iyya neighborhood of Gaza City in an armed confrontation with the IDF on 6 October. During this incident, an Israeli intelligence agent was also killed. The remaining two fugitives, Khalid Mahmud Salih and Ahmad al-Siftawi (son of As'ad al-Siftawi, a high-ranking Fatah leader in the Gaza Strip), managed to cross the border into Egypt.

Following the incident in Shaja'iyya, protest demonstrations were held in the Gaza Strip and student riots broke out at the Islamic University. In his Friday sermon in the al-Qassam Mosque, 'Awda lauded their acts and called on Palestinians to shake off hesitancy (*tamalmul*) and adopt the principle of martyrdom. Additionally, the Islamic Jihad published two leaflets: one, on 7 October, detailing the Shaja'iyya incident, the other on 9 October entitled: "My war is the death of martyrs." The leaflet called for protest strikes and demonstrations.[45]

Notably, the battle at Shaja'iyya occupies a place of honor in the narrative of the Islamic Jihad as the "spark" (al-sharara) that ignited the Intifada, when the fallen, in their death, manifested the ultimate self-sacrifice for Allah. According to the movement's Beirut-based organ, al-Mujahid:

> The six escapees had the opportunity to flee Palestine, but they refused, and justly so. Thus the choice was either life or death for the homeland. In their anti-Zionist activity, their eyes were always fixed forward to Palestine and to its holy heart, Jerusalem and the al-Aqsa Mosque. The 6th of October was the end of the period of submission and the start of the revival of the nation, which inevitably will spring from the soil on which the blessing of Allah rests.[46]

The rise in the number of attacks carried out by Islamic Jihad members in the Gaza Strip prompted the Israeli security authorities to take concerted action to destroy the movement's infrastructure. The fear (ultimately borne out) was that this brand of religious violence would be adopted by the large Islamic factor—the Brothers. Early in November 1987, dozens of high-ranking activists in the Islamic Jihad were arrested, including Ibrahim al-Najjar, Muhammad al-Hindi, 'Abdallah al-Sabi' and 'Abdallah al-Zaq. Shortly thereafter, an expulsion order was issued against 'Awda (15 November). The decision to expel 'Awda rather than imprison him stemmed from an awareness that prison served as a center for religious penitence and the recruitment of activists among the prisoners to the ranks of the Islamic Jihad. Imprisoning 'Awda together with Shiqaqi might only intensify this trend.[47] 'Awda's position as the imam of al-Qassam Mosque was assumed by Shaykh 'Abdallah al-Shami, a graduate of the Geography Department at the University of Zaqaziq in Egypt, who had served until then as a preacher in the al-Rahman Mosque in the Shaja'iyya neighborhood.[48]

'Awda denied the charges against him. In an interview with the East Jerusalem daily al-Fajr two days before his arrest, he stressed that he was not a leader or even a member of any organization whatsoever. Islam, he pointed out, was not a religion of violence or extremism, yet Muslims were commanded to fight against conquerors and their unjust deeds. He described the motif of jihad in Islam as "an act of self-defense."[49]

The decision to expel 'Awda, which was challenged by his attorney in Israel's Supreme Court, evoked rage and protest in several parts of the Gaza Strip. Some 300 students assembled on the Islamic University campus and declared a strike in solidarity with the arrested shaykh. A protest demonstration at the al-Qassam Mosque led to clashes with the security forces, and several persons were injured.[50] The strong support for 'Awda and his movement in the Gaza Strip was reflected in the results of the student council elections at the Islamic University in November 1987: the list identified with the Islamic Jihad gained 11% of the vote, in contrast to 4% the previous year.[51] Prior to the elections, Islamic Jihad activists conducted an aggressive campaign on campus, criticizing the Brothers for focusing excessively on education (*tarbiyya*) and neglecting jihad. A leaflet circulated in the Gaza Strip asserted:

> Jihad does not mean only the bearing of arms. Its real meaning is direct confrontation from the first moment that the heart perceives the truth of the uniqueness of Allah in the saying "There is no God but Allah." The form and means of this confrontation must be defined in accordance with the abilities to act. However, it is important that there should be no cease-fire or deferment.[52]

A new chapter in the history of the Islamic Jihad, and in the history of the Palestinians as a whole, began with the outbreak of the Intifada in early December 1987, which started as spontaneous rioting and gradually turned into an institutionalized activity.

The Intifada and the Shift of the Movement's Center to Lebanon and Syria (1988 onward)

The Intifada, which broke out on 9 December 1987, was essentially a popular uprising prompted by nationalist motivations and socioeconomic tensions. It also drew its vitality from Islam as an integral part of the cultural identity of the Palestinians. Islam, in the words of Sami Zubaida, served as an "ethnic marker"[53] drawing the boundaries of the Palestinian community as distinct from others identified by a different religion, i.e., Israel. This form of communal identification is supported by surveys and research carried out in the territories in the early 1970s and the first half of the 1980s, which showed that Islam remained the preferred model for social conduct for a majority of respondents. A survey of 2,000 Palestinians in the West Bank and the Gaza Strip published in September 1986 revealed that 55% of the respondents thought that the future Palestinian state should have some Islamic content, with 26% advocating a state based on the Shari'a. A strong religious tendency was especially noticeable among young educated residents of cities and refugee camps. In another sample, consisting of 388 students at al-Najah University in Nablus surveyed close to the outbreak of the Intifada, 40% of the respondents indicated that they led a religious way of life, while over 50% responded that an Islamic ideology seemed the most conducive to ending the occupation.[54] In this sense, the Intifada, which Emmanuel Sivan has called "an economic, societal and national convulsion,"[55] was also imbued with a significant measure of religiosity.

From the earliest stages of the Intifada, the leading role of the Islamic groups (i.e., Islamic Jihad and Hamas) was obvious in violent activity, in initiating demonstrations and in issuing leaflets, all of which aimed at dictating the daily agenda of the population. It was the Islamic Jihad that first published a leaflet (11 December 1987) calling on Palestinians to hold a general strike. The leaflet was signed for the first time by "The Islamic Jihad movement in Palestine," pointing to its intention to deviate from the narrow elitist, clandestine framework and become a broad popular movement.[56] This and other leaflets circulated during December 1987–January 1988 reflected the emphasis placed by the Islamic Jihad on its pioneering role (al-dawr al-ra'id) in paving the way for the outbreak of the Intifada.

In the event, however, the mantle of leadership in the Islamic camp in early 1988 clearly shifted to Hamas, the activist arm of the Brothers in the Gaza Strip, which had a broad and efficient civil network. The establishment of Hamas on the eve of the Intifada and its perpetration of violent acts against Israel reflected the process of "Palestinization" that had taken place in the Brothers' ranks during the 1970s and 1980s. It attested to the movement's acceptance of the order of priorities laid down by the Islamic

Jihad—"Liberated Palestine before Muslim Palestine."[57] The Islamic Jihad, with a membership of 2,000–4,000 in the Gaza Strip in late 1987,[58] now found itself in an inferior position. Two factors accounted for this: its semi-clandestine nature and limited resources; and the damage it sustained by the Israeli security forces (exposure of cells, arrests) and by the fact that its key leaders were either imprisoned (Shiqaqi, 'Awda) or resided outside the territories ('Aryan, Nafi', Shalah). These factors put it at a disadvantage in the competition with the PLO and Hamas over recruitment of members and the acquisition of influence.

Still, the importance of the Islamic Jihad did not lie in its organizational ability or political weight but in its success in entrenching militant Islam among Palestinians. Moreover, the movement's link with the Islamic camp, alongside Hamas, helped it maintain a reasonable scope of activity and elicit a high level of popular obedience to the directives of its leaflets.

Superficial and in some cases distorted press reports on the Islamic Jihad, and the PLO's disregard of its role in the outbreak of the Intifada, prompted the movement to issue a pamphlet in February 1988 clarifying its principles and its relationship with other Palestinian forces:

1. The Islamic Jihad is part of the Islamic trend in Palestine, which also includes the Brothers and the Liberation Party. It has a "political-popular rather than military character" and is not connected in any way with other groups active in the Arab world that use the same name.

2. The movement views the Palestinian problem as the central issue of the Islamic movement in Palestine and outside it, inasmuch as Israel personifies the "center of Western aggression against the Arab and Muslim world."

3. The movement maintains good ties with Fatah, which are "ties of standing in one front so long as it is aimed at the same enemy." The movement, however, is not represented in the United National Command (UNC), since the Intifada is an uprising of the Palestinian people, who are capable of deciding when "to advance and when to fall back, when to burn and when to attack with its stones and its bodies."[59]

The pamphlet reflected the Islamic Jihad's desire to retain its presence and influence in the Intifada, if only in the political sphere. In this it was partly successful. By contrast, the situation of the pro-Fatah Jihad groups in the West Bank had deteriorated. Dealing mainly with carrying out attacks, these groups were more vulnerable to exposure. A critical blow was delivered to the Islamic Jihad Squads when their commanders, Muhammad Basim al-Tamimi, Marwan al-Kiyali and Muhammad Bakhis, were killed in an explosion of a booby-trapped car in Limassol (February 1988). This incident, together with heightened monitoring by the Jordanian security services of contacts between the Jihad cells on the West Bank and their operators in Jordan, brought about a significant drop in the operational capacity of the faction.

Following the death of the Islamic Jihad Squads commanders, the Islamic Jihad circulated a leaflet lauding the three as heroes and emphasizing their devotion to Islam as taking precedence over any narrow political loyalties, i.e., to Fatah.[60] Concealing the fact that the three were Fatah activists and presenting them as products of revolutionary Islam were tactics aimed at giving the movement a renewed momentum. However, the Islamic Jihad remained far behind in matters related to conducting the Intifada.

The movement's position became still more problematic with the expulsion to Lebanon of its two key leaders, 'Awda (April 1988) and Shiqaqi (August 1988). These expulsions marked a shift in the movement's power base from the territories to Lebanon and Syria. Upon their arrival in Beirut, 'Awda and Shiqaqi met with officials of the Iranian Embassy and with Hizballah leaders. Their statements, which received wide coverage in the pro-Shi'i press, credited the Islamic Revolution as an important source of inspiration for the Intifada. They also clearly reflected the pro-Iranian orientation of the Islamic Jihad. Speaking at the Iranian Embassy in Beirut, 'Awda commented that the expulsion of leaders would not harm the progress of the Intifada, for "our entire people leads it." Moreover, the Intifada had proven "that Islam is a revolution, and that all the political trends emanate from the mosques."[61]

With the move to Lebanon and Syria, the ideological link of the Islamic Jihad to Iran as a revolutionary model was translated into a close political and organizational tie as well. This was manifested by logistic support received through the Iranian Embassy in Beirut and through Hizballah for the purpose of renewing armed anti-Israel activity, including attacks launched from the Lebanese border.[62] The Islamic Jihad focused its recruiting energies primarily on the population in the Palestinian refugee camps in Lebanon, and to a lesser degree on those in Syria

(given the sensitivity of the regime there). The refugee camps in Lebanon, especially 'Ayn al-Hilwa and Rushdiyya in Tyre and Sidon respec-
tively, were similar to those of the Gaza Strip in their societal composition. They served as fertile ground for Islamic indoctrination, for two reasons: the widespread economic distress in the camps, which worsened
further in the wake of the Lebanese War with the evacuation of PLO and
the rise of Shi'i elements in the local political scene; and the absence of
Palestinian Islamic movements, such as the Brothers, as a political factor
in Lebanon. This absence was particularly noticeable in view of the growing influence of the pro-Syrian Palestinian rejectionist groups there.[63]

In recruiting membership, the movement made use of Palestinian religious figures who held key posts in the refugee camps. They conducted
cultural activities emphasizing the Islamic dimension of the Intifada and
its link with the Islamic resistance in Lebanon. The leading figures in this
effort were Shaykhs 'Abdallah al-Haliq and Salim Mahmud al-Lababidi,
who were also the initiators of the establishment of the Supervisory Council for Religious Affairs in the refugee camps. Lababidi, who was known
for his close ties with the Iranian leaders and Shi'i groups in Lebanon,
soon became one of the leaders of the Islamic Jihad.[64]

Besides developing an infrastructure in Lebanon, Syria and other Arab
countries, including Sudan and Libya, the Islamic Jihad was active in
Western countries. There it made use of the democratic guarantees inherent in the freedoms of speech and assembly, and of the presence of substantial Palestinian communities in various locations. This task was
largely in the hands of the external leaders of the movement who were
pursuing higher education abroad and who carried out money transfers.
They were also engaging in publicist writing in Islamist journals. In particular, Bashir Nafi' wrote in al-'Alam (London) in the mid-1980s and later
in al-Insan (Paris). Britain and especially the US served as important
centers for Islamic forums and institutions. The most important of these
was the Tampa (Florida)-based Islamic Palestine Committee, which organized conferences and raised funds for Islamic activity related to the
Intifada. This forum was headed by Sami al-'Aryan, assisted by Ramadan
Shalah and Bashir Nafi', all three lecturers at the University of Southern
Florida.[65]

The explosion in the New York World Trade Center carried out by
Muslim extremists in 1993 prompted the federal authorities to tighten

surveillance regarding Islamic activity in the US. In January 1995, the White House issued an order freezing the American bank accounts of Arab-sponsored terror organizations. Arrest warrants were also issued for some of their leaders. The orders targeted Hizballah, Hamas and the Islamic Jihad, inter alia. A similar order was issued by Secretary of State Madeleine Albright in October 1997. These steps by the US, which were described by Shiqaqi as "a crusade against Islam,"[66] reduced Islamic Jihad activity in the US, but did not end it entirely.

While its main foci of activity were in the Arab and Western diaspora, the Islamic Jihad took care to demonstrate its ongoing presence in the territories and to maintain its links with its branches there. This was accomplished partly by means of messages and directives broadcast over a radio station in southern Syria—Radio al-Quds, controlled by Ahmad Jibril's Popular Front for the Liberation of Palestine—General Command (PFLP–GC).[67] Shiqaqi emphasized that the primary presence of the Islamic Jihad was in Palestine and that the base in Lebanon was created only after the expulsion of the movement's leaders. The presence in Syria, he pointed out, was limited and unofficial, and elsewhere even more insignificant.[68] Shiqaqi sought thereby to counter the derisive tone of both the PLO and Hamas toward what they regarded as the marginality of the Islamic Jihad in Palestinian politics and its dependence on outside elements. He also wanted to remove any doubt on the part of the Arab host countries over the existence of subversive activity in their territories.

Evidence of the success of the movement in keeping up its activity on the ground was provided by an attack on a passenger bus on the road to Jerusalem, and stabbings in Tel Aviv (April, May 1989). These attacks elicited large-scale arrests of movement members for possession of arms and perpetrating attacks against Israeli targets. Notable detainees included Jamil 'Ulyan, Muhammad al-Hindi, Khalid al-Shaykh 'Ali, Yusuf 'Arif and Ahmad Abu Daqa. Political activity was also sustained, focusing on campuses. Moreover, the mass expulsion to Lebanon in 1992 of 50 of the movement's activists, including 'Abdallah al-Shami and 'Abdallah al-Zaq, together with approximately 350 Hamas figures, pointed to the preservation of its relative status in the context of Islamic activity in the territories.[69]

In the movement's view, an active front against Israel both in Palestine and simultaneously from Lebanon constituted an accurate interpretation of the principle of jihad, which required a struggle to the end against the Jews "from the north to the south."[70] As a result of its physical proximity to Hizballah in Lebanon, the Islamic Jihad established a military wing, *Sayf al-Islam* (The Sword of Islam), represented by a military spokesman, with units named for martyrs of the movement. The name of the military wing was later changed to *al-Qasam* (The Oath). The movement also began publishing a weekly, *al-Mujahid*, based in Beirut and distributed throughout the Arab world. A recurrent theme in all of its publications was the importance of acquiring technological expertise and organizational efficiency in order to empower and advance the jihad in Palestine.[71]

Another aspect was the formation of an internal structure with three tiers. They were, in ascending order: a general congress (*mu'tamar 'amm*), which included members from the territories and the Arab diaspora; an advisory council (*majlis shura*); and a general secretariat (*amana 'amma*), headed by Shiqaqi. According to Nafidh 'Azzam, the *shura* (consultation) was the main pillar of the movement, with decision-making taking place within this framework. In the same vein, the movement's internal charter emphasized the decentralized character of its leadership, which was elected and was allowed freedom of opinion. Underlying these statements was the desire to imbue the Islamic Jihad with a democratic image, and thereby also to expand its ranks. Conditions for acceptance in the movement included a general commitment to Islam, righteousness, and adherence to the movement's political platform. A member who behaved immorally was to be expelled from the movement, or suspended for a period to be determined by the seriousness of his offense.[72]

Like Hamas, the Islamic Jihad opened its doors to women. It viewed the woman as an axis of liberation from the values of *jahiliyya*. Its spokesmen expressed support for women's involvement in the political and social struggle in Palestine, yet subordinated them to Islamic restrictions and assigned them marginal roles in the movement's institutions. Women were also required to wear a veil. One of the noted women in the Islamic Jihad was 'Atif 'Ulyan of Bethlehem, who headed the *al-Niqa'* (Purity) charitable association there and was imprisoned in Israel for nine years (1988–96) for subversive activity.[73] Like Hamas, too, the movement accepted Christians, who were permitted to retain their faith and customs, although they were required to adopt the political line of the movement and refrain from committing any serious infraction of the laws of Islam. In practice, few Christians joined the movement, and those who did eventually converted to Islam.[74]

Similar conditions for acceptance were to be found in other factions of the Palestinian Islamic Jihad. The main emphasis in all of them, however, was placed on the authoritative status of the leader, who, in the functions he assumed, personified the role of the Prophet as religious teacher, politician and military commander during the formative period of Islam. The members of the movement owed him absolute loyalty and submissive obedience in the form of an oath of allegiance *(bay'a)*.[75]

With the protraction of the Intifada, the ideological gap between the Islamic Jihad and Hamas effectively narrowed. The entry of Hamas into the circle of armed struggle against Israel, and the Palestinian coloration which it adopted (especially with the publication of its charter in 1988), were viewed by the Islamic Jihad as an important development. With this, Islamic Jihad began to distance itself from Fatah, while displaying a positive attitude toward the Palestinian left, which, despite its Marxist platform, remained faithful to the path of armed struggle. The fact that some of the leftist groups maintained a close connection with Iran and the Shi'i groups in Lebanon also contributed to the tactical convergence between them and the Islamic Jihad.

Chapter Two:
Ideological Outlook

"Israel was born to die. It did not arrive in the region
in order to stay, but to leave."

—*al-Tali'a al-Islamiyya*, March 1983

The ideological outlook of the Islamic Jihad has been at once traditional and revolutionary: traditional in rejecting the prevailing sociopolitical order in the Arab world in favor of a perceived Islamic golden age; and revolutionary in denouncing the approach of Islamic circles regarding the timing of jihad in Palestine. A central pillar has been setting Palestine free by means of violent and immediate struggle.

In spite of its explicit Palestinian dimension, however, the Islamic Jihad has not had a fixed or cohesive platform. Rather, it has blended themes deriving from three main sources: the ideology of the Muslim Brothers, as developed especially by Sayyid Qutb; the ideological guidelines and patterns of activity of the Islamic militant groups in Egypt; and the Islamic Revolution in Iran. An additional historic source of inspiration, especially in the area of organization, has been the armed struggle of religious figures against the Jewish and the British presence in Palestine during the 1930s and 1940s, led by Shaykh 'Izz al-Din al-Qassam. Qassam is depicted in Islamic Jihad writings as the harbinger of revolutionary activism in Palestine, a far cry from the hesitant behavior of the traditional leadership at that time.[1]

The absence of firm ideological underpinnings, pointing to a degree of intellectual superficiality, has been reflected in Islamic Jihad's focus on the political aspect of Islam, while eschewing social and economic issues of concern to the Palestinians and to Muslims generally. In the movement's view, these issues are products of Western-Zionist aggression, and resolving them is conditional solely on political and military acts to wipe out this aggression. Shiqaqi, in a somewhat apologetic argument, observed that his movement's social and economic platform is anchored in the holy text and in Muslim history, as well as in cumulative human experience that does not conflict with Islam. A more concrete argument was given by Ramadan Shalah. He pointed out that the movement focuses on politics and military operations, in line with its ideological motto of immediate struggle against the occupation, especially since, unlike the Brothers, it lacks the material resources to advance evolutionary change in society.[2]

The Palestine Problem and the Islamic Nation

According to the Islamic Jihad, a proper reading of the Qur'an and an understanding of history would lead to the unequivocal conclusion that Palestine is at the focus of the religio-historic confrontation between the Muslims and their eternal enemies, the Jews. The Muslims represent the forces of truth (al-haqq), while the Jews (and the Christians), the forces of apostasy (al-batil). Beyond its Qur'anic dimension—the sacredness of Jerusalem for Muslims after that of Mecca and Medina—Palestine serves as an important geopolitical axis that links three continents and thus con-stitutes "the Muslims' most important homeland." The recognition of Palestine as the most vital point in the Muslim world had led the West to focus its drive for destroying Islam on it.[3] The allies of the West in pursu-ing this goal were the Jews. 'Awda, relying on citations from the Qur'an relating to the Jews (especially in the al-Isra' and al-Baqara suras), noted that the Qur'an warned the Muslims of the great danger personified by the Jews, who are the enemies of Islamic civilization.[4]

The origin of the Palestinian problem, in this narrative, goes back to a Western offensive that began with Napoleon's invasion of Egypt (1798) and reached a climax with the disbanding of the Ottoman Empire (1918), which had symbolized the "unity of the Islamic nation." The collapse of the empire turned the Muslims into strangers in their own land. Local elites who joined forces with the crusader West against the Ottomans and became the rulers of Iraq, Syria, Lebanon and Egypt, belonged to a nar-row segment that was isolated from the people and distant from the prob-lem of Palestine. The ideological and political displacement of Islam was accomplished at the instigation of liberal and socialist Arab regimes.

Politicians and thinkers who espoused liberal nationalism, the Islamic Jihad noted, erred in two ways by turning to the West: they identified

European history with the history of mankind generally; and they acted to eliminate their own heritage, wherein lay the capacity for collective renewal. They failed to understand that the West was not truly interested in the advancement of humanity, but rather in dominating it. The "achievements" of the liberal experience in the Middle East were two-fold: destroying the caliphate, and accelerating the process that led to the establishment of Israel in the heart of the Muslim homeland. Despite the momentum that the Islamic movement gathered under Hasan al-Banna during the 1930s and 1940s, it did not succeed in becoming a viable alternative to secular liberalism due to its relatively brief experience. The military regimes which had emerged in the 1950s represented a more radical version of Western nationalism, and proved to be enemies of Islam and its exponents.[5] Since the source of both the liberal and the military regimes was "the Western impulse," they failed to attain true independence and social justice, or to liberate Palestine. This failure was revealed in all its severity in the wake of the Arab defeats of 1948 and 1967, as reflected in the following analysis by the Islamist writer Tawfiq al-Tayyib, who was often quoted by the Islamic Jihad:

> The non-Islamic leaderships...which took over governance after the defeat of the Ottoman state at the start of the 20th century, represented the consistent retreat in the face of the Zionist-Western challenge that seeks to cancel out history, undermine the Islamic identity, and take control of the land. The failure of these leaderships in 1948 and later in 1967, and their impotence in continuing the armed struggle against Israel, were a direct result of their inability to comprehend the religious essence of the struggle.[6]

Tayyib declared that only Islam had the power to restore inner balance to Muslim society and liberate it from its inferior status vis-à-vis the West. However, the return to Islam would not be complete without making Palestine the highest priority of the Islamic movements. "Palestine is the future criterion for Islam and the Arab people. It will determine whether this faith will be destroyed or will survive, whether this people will live or be lost," Tayyib wrote.[7] The existence of subservient and secular Arab regimes, and the entrenchment of the Zionist entity in the heart of the Muslim region, facilitate the struggle of Western imperialism against the restoration of Islam in politics. As a result, Muslim society remains in a condition of fragmentation and ideological degeneration.[8] In such a climate, 'Awda observed, the problem of Palestine lost its uniqueness, a process aided by the shallow approach of Islamic movements and the PLO.

Spokesmen for the Muslim Brothers, along with 'ulama', viewed Israel as a vexing problem whose origin lay in a more general problem—the absence of the caliphate. In their view, an effective confrontation with Israel was possible only after the establishment of a larger Islamic state. As proof, they cited the Prophet's historic undertaking of jihad only after 13 years of preaching in Mecca. The Islamic movement, these spokesmen held, was now in the Mecca phase, which was a stage for building rather than confrontation, patience rather than jihad.

Rejecting this view, the Islamic Jihad claimed that it was erroneous for two reasons. First, the Mecca phase was not free of strife. On the contrary, it was a period of one of the most pronounced ideological struggles ever, during which Islam and its believers were challenged by ignorance and heresy. The confrontation between truth and falsehood that occurred was part of the crystallization of Islamic identity. Second, the molding of Islam and the compilation of the Shari'a had long since been completed. The duty of Muslims was now to fulfill Allah's will. How, for example, could the advocates of the Mecca-phase argument justify their pronounced support for the Afghan fighters? Those brave fighters did not dwell on the question of whether they had passed the Meccan or Medinan phase, but raised the banner of jihad without hesitation against the conquerors of their land. While education and patience were indeed important in every age, once Muslim faith and land have been threatened by destruction, there is no alternative to firm resistance against imperialism and its regional allies. In reality, whenever Islamic movements moved from confrontation with despotic rulers to a cease-fire and even participation in governance, they did not advance the vision of establishing an Islamic state. On the contrary, their supporters were forced into a defensive, siege-like position.[9]

A similar fate was in store for the PLO, which viewed the struggle against Israel in geographic terms far removed from its religio-historic context. As a result, the PLO became a mere a tool for Arab regimes, who subjected it to cruel blows, as those inflicted by Husayn in the Black September incidents in Jordan (1970), by Syria in the Lebanon arena (1975 onward), and by Sadat following the Camp David Accords (1978).[10]

Given the fragile position of Muslim society in the 20th century, Shiqaqi argued, the Islamic option gained force by virtue of the historic fact that "for generations, Islam was the pathway to the nation's rising up from defeat." A notable example was Turkey, stronghold of secularism in the Middle East, which, despite the repressive nullification of its heritage by a secular regime, "chose Islam once again."[11] From the 1960s onward, Islamist thinkers, such as Sayyid Qutb in Egypt, Malik bin Nabi in Algeria or 'Ali Shari'ati in Iran, vigorously defined the boundary between Islam and heresy. They laid out the features of a just Islamic society, and pointed out that "religion must possess reverence and power which will strike fear into the forces of tyranny."[12] However, the transition from a reformist to a revolutionary approach, fueled by the waves of religious revival of the 1970s, did not signal any substantial change in the attitude toward the rightful place of Palestine within the overall struggle against the West and Israel. This change became the province of the Palestinian Jihad, which Shiqaqi crowned as "the pioneer who leads the camp."[13]

Inasmuch as the Jewish presence in Palestine serves as a palpable symbol of Muslim inferiority in the modern age, the commitment to Palestine cannot be framed in the narrow context of Palestinian or Arab nationalism. The Palestinian problem, the movement argued, is a purely Islamic issue, and this is the key "to every serious strategy aimed at the liberation and unification of the Muslim nation." It is here that the Islamic Jihad's ideological innovation lies, i.e., raising the flag of jihad in Palestine involves a commitment to two interrelated goals: the liberation of Palestine and a pan-Islamic revival in the region.[14] The failure of the Islamic trends—both traditional and radical—to position the Palestinian cause as their top priority constitutes a denial of the unique position of Palestine in the Qur'an and in Muslim history. It also removes millions of Muslims from the struggle against Israel and its patron, the West.[15]

The Islamic Jihad recognized that the Arab regional reality, characterized by factionalism and by divergence from Islam, forced Islamic groups to focus their energies on domestic issues and detracted from their ability to offer substantive aid to the jihad fighters in Palestine. These groups, however, were required to direct every achievement in the strategy of change in their countries to promoting the goal of the liberation of Palestine. The nature of the struggle could vary from capital to capital, e.g., political and educational activity in Amman, or armed jihad in Cairo, but no armistice with the existing regimes was permissible. Otherwise, the result would be divergence from the Islamic goal that calls for Muslim unity. The pinnacle of Islamic activity outside Palestine, 'Awda argued, is "the establishment of an Islamic liberation army that will undertake the decisive campaign."[16] With the restoration of Palestine to its lawful masters, the Jews will be placed once again under the dominion of Islam, which, viewed historically, assured their physical and spiritual existence better than did Christian Europe.[17]

These Islamic Jihad arguments reveal a painful recognition that the main burden, at least in the initial stage, falls on the Muslims of Palestine alone. Despite the limited resources at their disposal, they are compelled to mount the jihad against Israel immediately because their country is under direct occupation. The enemy seeks to destroy their authentic Islamic identity and turn their land into a "bridgehead for war against the rest of the Muslim countries."[18] The duty of jihad and martyrdom is imposed on every Palestinian who is sound in spirit and body (*fard 'ayn*). Jihad in its broad meaning must be turned both inward (establishing a just Islamic society) and outward (against the heretical occupation). Adopting it is the sole criterion for testing the adherence of the believer to Islam. It prevents the formation of a spiritual vacuum by which the enemy seeks to establish his presence in Palestine, and fuels Islam's external struggle against the West and its local dependents.[19]

The sanctification of jihad in Palestine, which means the presence of the Palestinians at the forefront of the battle, is founded on religio-historic determinism that promises the victory of truth (the Muslims) over falsehood and apostasy (the Jews). It is a struggle that is devoid of compromises, relating to the fate of belief in Allah. Although the present balance of power does not favor the Muslims, they must find breaches, and even remain silent for a time so as to avoid becoming only partially enfranchised. According to 'Awda, the superiority of the Jews, with the backing of the West, is fleeting and anomalous (*wad' istithna'i*). It does not reflect the normative situation, as was manifested in the formative age of Islam, in which the Jews were fated to be a degraded element because of their failure to realize their divine mission. They coalesced into a collective entity and gained political status only from the 19th century onward, with the shrinking of Islam as a political power. The historic continuity of Islamic resistance, however, was never cut off. It was nurtured by revival movements such as the Wahhabiyya in the Arabian Peninsula, the Sanusiyya in Libya and the Mahdiyya in Sudan, and by charismatic figures such as Jamal al-Din al-Afghani, Hasan al-Banna and Sayyib Qutb. This continuity reached a peak with the Islamic Revolution in Iran in 1979.[20]

The Islamic Revolution in Iran

The Islamic Jihad viewed the Islamic Revolution in Iran as a major historic link in the Muslim struggle against modern Western attempts to exclude Islam from politics. The Iranian experiment was distinctive in admitting the masses into the political process, and in its success in establishing a state founded on Shari'a and led by jurists (*wilayat al-faqih*). This success, according to Shiqaqi, stemmed from several factors. One was the entrenched position of the religious authorities in society. Another was the revolutionary message calling for jihad, going beyond civic and cultural struggle, as espoused by the Brothers in the Arab states. Yet another factor was self-criticism, carried on in Islamic circles during the pre-revolutionary period, which fortified the bonds with the masses and produced a political platform for solving the problems faced by Muslims in modern times. If the Islamic movements in the Arab world wanted to free themselves from ideological distortion and advance comprehensive change in society, Shiqaqi urged, they had to adopt internal dialogue and self-criticism as a basic criterion of everyday activity.[21]

The overthrow of the Shah in Iran, besides symbolizing the first modern victory of Islam over the West, proved to Muslims that change was not only possible, but also preordained. It provided concrete refutation of the damaging thesis put forward by local Westernized intellectuals that Islam was a spiritual resource and a psychological need "incapable of governance." Shiqaqi praised Khomeini's vigorous policy, upon taking power, of curbing the theft of the country's resources by foreign companies and establishing a new political system that carries on an intimate dialogue with the people.[22] In this context, Iran constituted the antithesis to heretical Arab regimes which serve as a tool for the West in weakening adherence to Islam.

The disintegration of the Ottoman Empire marked the severance of Islam from the helm of political leadership and the introduction of the separation between religion and state. The Arab governments enforced this principle in order to enhance the people's political subservience and perpetuate its fragmentation. Fear of the return of Islam to the political arena elicited a hostile reaction on the part of the Arab leaders to the Islamic Revolution and its messages. This was confirmed, in 'Awda's view, by the Iran-Iraq War, which broke out in 1980, and the *hajj* incident of July 1987, during which some 400 Iranian pilgrims were killed by Saudi security forces.[23]

In the view of the Islamic Jihad, the Iranian revolution not only constitutes an ideal model for Muslims, but also represents the start of a process of Islamization throughout the region and a vital step toward restoring the caliphate. Shiqaqi praise Khomeini's approach of adopting jihad as a symbol of political activism and defying the quietist Shi'i tradition that justifies dissimulation (*taqiyya*) until the appearance of the anticipated mahdi. Jihad under Iran's leadership, he added, has both a defensive and an aggressive character and strives to advance the struggle of all the oppressed (*al-mustad'afin*) against the forces of evil and tyranny (*al-mustakbirin*).[24]

The Islamic Jihad sought to repress the problematic aspects of the Sunni-Shi'i relationship by focusing on the essential similarities between Sunni and Shi'i law regarding the belief in Allah and His Prophet, the Qur'an, the five pillars of Islam and the resurrection of the dead. This involved downplaying historical resentments and ideological disputes, such as the bloody conflict between the House of 'Ali and its opponents over the caliphate; the Shi'is' eschatological myths relating to the return of the Hidden Imam to restore justice on earth under 'Ali's descendants; and the self-image of the Shi'i 'ulama' as substitutes for the Hidden Imam in guiding the community. This last issue came to ahead when Khomeini instituted the concept of governance by the Muslim jurisprudent.

In Shiqaqi's opinion, efforts by Arab regimes to batter the Iranian Revolution by inflaming the hostility between Sunna and Shi'a distort the historic truth and only serve Western imperialism. The degree of division between the two factions of Islam is much less than that between Sunna and *Mu'tazila* (a theological school advocating a rational-philosophic approach to faith); yet, no religio-legal authority ever ruled against a Mu'tazili caliph. For example, Caliph al-Ma'mun (813–33) continued to elicit obedience despite the torture of Imam Ahmad Ibn Hanbal under his rule. Moreover, while the writings of important Sunni thinkers such as Banna and Qutb received media coverage in Iran, Khomeini took care to emphasize Muslim unity. Not surprisingly, Khomeini elicited praise from highly placed Islamic figures in the Sunni world, such as Shaykh al-Azhar 'Abd al-Halim Mahmud, Abu al-A'la Mawdudi and various Brothers leaders. Vigorous steps taken by Khomeini in late 1982 against Sunni elements in Iran, such as Shaykh 'Uthman al-Naqshbandi, one of the leaders of the Sufi orders, and Shaykh Ahmad Mufti Zada, a Kurdish leader, were devoid of religious or ethnic motivation. They were aimed purely at eliminating manifestations of social exploitation and the disturbance of public order, said Shiqaqi.[25]

In adopting an ecumenical approach toward the Shi'a, and highlighting Khomeini's pan-Islamic vision, Shiqaqi sought to bring about a dialogue between Iran and the Sunni radicals in order to fend off the Western-Jewish threat. A similar stance was taken by another Palestinian Islamist, Shaykh As'ad Bayyud al-Tamimi. In a *fatwa* issued in the territories in 1985, Tamimi declared that the Shi'is did not preach division in Islam, for they held up the same Qur'an and prayed to Mecca in the same way as other Muslims. What was important was to cooperate with the Islamic Revolution and avoid theological polemics over the essence of Shi'a.[26]

In searching for religious backing for the integral status of Shi'a in Islam, Shiqaqi delved into the writings of medieval and modern Muslim thinkers considered prestigious in the Sunni world. He held that the hostility toward Shi'a shown by Ibn Taymiyya (d. 1328) was not directed at the Twelver Shi'ism, which dominated Iran, but only at the extremist Isma'ili and 'Alawite factions. He also referred to a *fatwa* issued by Shaykh Mahmud Shaltut of al-Azhar (d. 1963), which recognized the Shi'a as the fifth school in Muslim law—the Ja'farite School (named after the Sixth Imam Ja'far al-Sadiq).[27] Shiqaqi's reliance, inter alia, on Ibn Taymiyya and on Shaltut in order to gain radical Sunni sympathy for Shi'i Iran was problematic. Ibn Taymiyya, an important source of inspiration for Sunni radicals, did indeed defy the Imamate Twelver Shi'a—the mainstream of Shi'ism. His obsessive concern about removing every possible danger to the purity of the faith presented by deviant Muslims obscured the subtle distinctions between the various Shi'i branches and tarnished the Shi'a in its entirely by Sunni delegitimation. One of his *fatwas* held that the Shi'a, like the Kharijites, introduced the first *bid'a* (false innovation) in Islam by turning against a legitimate caliph, scheming against believers, and neglecting the Qur'an and the Sunna.[28]

Mahmud Shaltut, for his part, belonged to the establishment 'ulama', whose legal authority was rejected by the radicals on the grounds that the 'ulama' were merely submissive functionaries of the state. Shaltut, in his high post as shaykh al-Azhar, also served as chief spokesman of the Nasserist regime, thereby granting religious approval to the policy of persecution it adopted against the Muslim Brothers.[29]

Shiqaqi was aware of the theological and political difficulties in recruiting Sunni traditions to reinforce his ecumenical approach to the Shi'a. The strategy that he adopted of ignoring these difficulties or minimizing their importance did not help much in defusing the tensions between the two established historical narratives—the Sunna and the Shi'a. Moreover, his readiness to recognize Khomeini as the central political authority in the Muslim world distanced many of his Sunni colleagues, who jealously preserved their independence and viewed themselves, and not Khomeini, as a political alternative to the existing Arab regimes. Their de facto recognition of the political boundaries in the Arab Middle East also dictated their opposition to any submission to a central Islamic rule, much less a Shi'i one. As a consequence, Shiqaqi's ecumenism remained an intellectual exercise.

The Islamic Jihad indeed expressed disappointment with this equivocal, and even hostile, Sunni response to the Islamic Revolution, but attributed it to the intensive propaganda campaign mounted by Arab regimes to denigrate the Islamic Revolution. This double siege of Iran—Arab and Western—prevented the coalescence of the Middle East into an important Islamic bloc that could play a central role in international politics, in Shiqaqi's view.[30]

Shiqaqi hoped to build a broader Sunni consensus around the Islamic Revolution, by means of emphasizing the Palestinian element of Khomeini's policy. He pointed out that despite the geographic distance,

Khomeini treated the Palestinian issue as an internal problem, reflecting his awareness that the struggle of Islam against Western culture existed not only on the ideological plane but in a physical clash with Israel. In his view, the danger of Israel was manifested both in its takeover of the Muslim holy places and in its expansionist conduct, aimed at realizing the Zionist vision of the "kingdom of the universe."[31] Following this approach, Khomeini supported reinforcing the PLO and placing the goal of the liberation of Jerusalem at the top of Iran's priorities. This commitment to Palestine was anchored in two manifestos he published during the 1973 war and in a *fatwa* he issued during the Islamic Revolution, in which he urged the Muslim countries to allocate financial and material resources to destroy the Jewish entity.[32]

The halfhearted Arab response to Iran's anti-Zionist line was conspicuous, 'Abdallah al-Shami charged. The Arab leaders, seeking to remove the Palestinian problem from their public agenda, systematically repressed the Islamic groups in their countries. Indeed, Shami noted, while other peoples made contributions to humanity in important areas, e.g., Europeans in fathering the industrial revolution and the Japanese in the communications revolution, the Arabs were stagnant. This, he stated, was a consequence of political despotism that turned its back on human welfare and freedom.[33]

This pronounced anti-Arab tone was well reflected in the movement's unequivocal support for Iran in its war against Iraq (1980–88). Islamic Jihad leaders castigated Saddam Husayn's repressive regime for carrying out widespread arrests and executing Islamists during the war, including the Shi'i Imam Muhammad Baqir al-Sadr. They also accused Saddam of recruiting Arab and Western states to help him protect his oil resources and to take revenge on Khomeini for overthrowing the Shah. Saddam believed that Iran would collapse under the siege along its borders, Shiqaqi observed, but its people displayed an impressive capacity for resistance, nurtured by a strong belief in the victory of Islam. This resistance, similar to that of the jihad fighters against the Soviet Union in Afghanistan, and to Hizballah against Israel in Lebanon, was an important source of inspiration for the Palestinians, and fueled the eruption of the Intifada in 1987.[34]

The Intifada

The Intifada is described in Islamic Jihad literature as a "revolution" (*thawra*), rather than a spontaneous uprising (*intifada 'afuiyya*). It became a fixed phenomenon in the lives of the Palestinians, viewed by the movement as yet another phase of the historic Islamic struggle against the Jewish presence in Palestine. By emphasizing historic continuity and using religious anti-Jewish terminology, the movement sought to highlight the religious content of the conflict in Palestine, which for many years had been overshadowed by the dominant nationalist-secular stance.[35]

The adherence to Islam gathered momentum as a result of two important developments in the Palestinian and regional arenas from the mid-1970s onward: first, Palestinian disappointment with the nationalist-secular platform; and second, the victories attained by Islamic forces in Afghanistan, Iran, Egypt and Lebanon, which once more confirmed the vitality of Islam as a political force.[36] These two developments served as an impetus to crystallize a revolutionary trend in the territories based on three main tenets: Islam as an ideological and cultural basis; Palestine as a central goal; and jihad as a means to liberate Palestine and remove the Western threat from the Muslim nation.[37]

The movement left no room for doubt about the Islamic identity of the Intifada:

> The revolution has one address, which is the revolution of the Palestinians, and the Palestinians have one address—their identity as Muslims....It is only fitting that the blessed Intifada be free of the narrow party goals and the claims of ownership of it from here and there. Suffice it to say that this is entirely a people's revolution which adheres to Islam.[38]

Side by side with emphasizing the Islamic and the popular dimension of the Intifada, the Islamic Jihad extolled its own distinguished role in paving the way for its outbreak. The year that preceded the Intifada was termed by Shiqaqi "the year of Islam" in light of the active Islamic presence in the political and military spheres.[39] However, the claim that Islamic Jihad had paved the way for the outbreak of the Intifada, Shiqaqi explained, did not mean that it had a monopoly over the course of the

Intifada, nor did it deny the historic role of other Palestinian political forces—the PLO and the Brothers. PLO factions demonstrated opposition to the Israeli occupation, while the Brothers filled an educational role in returning the people to Islam. Still, "the Intifada broke out with blood shed by Islamic Jihad martyrs. Later, other forces joined it."[40]

The Intifada yielded a number of impressive achievements by exposing the fragility of Israeli society in the face of a popular uprising whose main weapons consisted of determination and stones; by restoring the 'ulama' and the mosques to their political and social leadership roles; by reducing the dependence of the local population on services and goods originating in the Israeli economy; and by shifting the Palestinian problem from the marginal status it had been assigned for years to center stage, regionally and internationally.[41] These accomplishments, "which had not been achieved by Palestinian efforts for decades," Shiqaqi pointed out, were attained in a short period.[42]

Still, the movement voiced disappointment with the failure of the Intifada in attaining the other objective of Palestinian jihad: a pan-Islamic revival in the rest of the Arab world. The reason for this failure, according to Shiqaqi, was the Arab leaders' fear of the sweeping nature of the uprising, which was aimed essentially at the Western imperialist allies in the Middle East—Israel and the Arab states. This fear was well reflected in both the official and the popular Arab stance, which ranged from hesitancy to merely verbal support of the heroic struggle of the Palestinians. Only in two capitals in the Middle East, Tehran and Beirut, was vigorous support for the Intifada demonstrated without fear of repression by the authorities.[43] Mass demonstrations held periodically in these two capitals expressed an awareness that it was the fighters in Palestine who "defended the last Islamic wall—Jerusalem and its surroundings."[44]

In the view of the Islamic Jihad, the linear progression of the Intifada toward the longed-for liberation of Palestine would not necessarily be free of digressions, although these would be essentially temporary. A notable example was the PLO success in rebounding from its shock at the start of the Intifada, and utilizing its achievements as a bargaining chip to attain concessions from Israel. Shiqaqi cited several factors accounting for this success by the PLO:

1. The inability of the Palestinian Islamic camp to consolidate a clear political program or establish a unified leadership as a preliminary con-

dition for recruiting the public. This failure limited its influence in the Intifada and allowed the PLO to eclipse it by establishing the UNC as a coordinating body for the nationalist factions. Shiqaqi hinted at criticism of Hamas for rejecting the hand of unity extended to it by Islamic Jihad, and for evading the need to provide a concrete Islamic response to Palestinian aspirations.

2. The PLO's effective financial and propaganda infrastructure, which helped it project the Intifada to the Palestinians at large as dovetailing with its own narrow political interests.

3. The material and financial assistance granted the PLO by the Arab regimes in order to tighten their hold on the organization and route it toward a political compromise. By contrast, the Islamic movements in the Arab world were content to issue declarations of support with no real content, attesting to their distorted order of priorities.[45]

Shiqaqi pointed out, however, that the temporary superiority of the PLO did not reflect the prevailing mood of the Palestinians, who believed that defiant opposition to the West would wipe out Israel by virtue of Islam only. Moreover, the PLO itself was in trouble internally because of disagreement in its ranks over the future of the Intifada and the issue of political settlement. In order to restore the Intifada to its long-term strategic goals, a thorough house-cleaning within the Islamic movements both in Palestine and outside was required.[46] This would engender the consolidation of a political program based on three avenues of action: sustaining the resistance to the Zionist enemy so as to erode its powers; removing the existing Arab regimes both by violent means and by communal activity aimed at strengthening civil society vis-à-vis the state; and cultivating ties with Islamic forces in the Third World in order to expand the struggle against the West and its allies.[47]

In forging a close link between Islamic activity in Palestine and in the Arab-Muslim world, the Islamic Jihad sought to highlight the pan-Islamic idea, but also to acquire strategic depth with material and human resources in order to promote the particularist Islamist agenda in Palestine.

The issue of unity among opposition groups in the Middle East was posited by the Islamic Jihad as another important goal, based on its view that the struggle against external enemies had priority over internal disputes. In this context, Shiqaqi referred to cooperation between three trends that in the past had been involved in direct confrontation with each other and by the 1980s had become relatively ineffective: the Islamic trend, weakened by repressive measures taken against it and the denigration of its image as terrorist; the pan-Arab trend, weakened by the thwarted vision of Arab unity and the threat of Israeli economic expansion; and the democratic trend, weakened by the dictatorial nature of Arab regimes. Each of these trends constituted a social force that could not be discounted or eliminated from public activity. Cooperation between them would erode the strength of local regimes and heighten popular recruitment on behalf of Palestine.[48]

In placing the Palestinian cause at the top of its agenda, the Islamic Jihad stressed that there was no significant contradiction between Islam and Arab nationalism, or between Islam and democracy in the sense of protecting human rights. First, Islam did not conspire against the distinctiveness of peoples, especially Arabs, who spread the faith throughout the world and were destined to play a key role in Muslim revival in modern times. Second, Islam respected the will of the nation and favored broad political participation based on the *shura*, which was a divine commandment and not only a human privilege. It sanctioned the institutions and means that advanced human rights, but rejected the Western interpretation of democracy, which views the people as the source of authority and legislation. This last view was defective, for the method of elections in the West actually prevented popular participation: the public voted only once every four years, and even then voter turnout was less than 50%. In Islam, by contrast, Allah was the sovereign and His authority was manifested in the Shari'a, which regulated human conduct.[49] As Shiqaqi, quoting Sayyid Qutb, put it: "The Muslim has no identity save that of his faith."[50]

Clearly, in the movement's outlook, Arab nationalism, as well as democracy, do not have an independent *raison d'être* but rather are subservient to the promotion of Islamic goals. Arab nationalism is legitimate only so long as it is confined to the context of the unity of faith, while democracy is legitimate only when viewed within an Islamic and not a Western context, and only if it functions within the confines of Shari'a authority. Not surprisingly, in return for recognition of their legitimacy, these other trends were required to divest themselves of the secular notion of the separation of religion and state, and the view of religion as ritual only. They must acknowledge the superior status of Islam as "a belief and a way of life" and as "the primary force leading the struggle against the West."[51] The Islamic Jihad's internal charter went one step further by stating that "the Islamic movement is the sole spokesman of the Muslim peoples and the authentic alternative to the infidel regimes."[52] In contrast to the movement's ecumenical approach to the Shi'a, which fostered close and equitable relations between Shi'is and Sunnis, its approach to the non-Islamic trends in the Arab world was based on the a priori superiority of Islam.

Indeed, the underscoring of unity over divisiveness, which was given expression in various conferences attended by the Islamic Jihad in the Arab diaspora,[53] reflected political pragmatism rather than ideological compromise regarding the role of Islam in shaping society. It was also the principle that dictated the relations of the movement with other forces in Palestinian politics.

Chapter Three:
Between the PLO and the Brothers/Hamas

Islamic Jihad-PLO Relations

The religious tide in the territories during the early 1980s, and the emergence of the Islamic Jihad, focused Palestinian public debate on the political—rather than cultural—aspect of Islam. The PLO, whose infrastructure in Lebanon was destroyed by Israel in 1982 and whose focus of activity shifted inward to the territories, was eager to absorb religious militancy into its national struggle. It had two objectives in this effort: to prevent radical Islam from becoming an attractive alternative to Palestinian nationalism; and, more specifically, to erode the strength of the Brothers and their chief organ in the Gaza Strip, *al-Mujamma'*.

Toward this end, the PLO leadership adopted a two-track strategy: operatively, the formation of clandestine Jihad cells with a pro-Fatah orientation, whose members saw little contradiction between national and religious activism; and politically, a wider use of Islamic rhetoric in official conclaves of PLO bodies and in its leaders' statements. A mark of the PLO's desire for religious legitimacy was its choice of Shaykh 'Abd al-Hamid al-Sa'ih as chairman of the Palestinian National Council (PNC), which first convened in Amman in April 1987 (albeit without the participation of the Palestinian left).[1] Sa'ih, a respected religious figure who had served in the past as president of the Supreme Muslim Council in Jerusalem and was expelled to Jordan in 1967, provided 'Arafat with a model of an official Islam subservient to, or at least in harmony with, Palestinian national goals.

The steps taken by 'Arafat to deal with the Islamic challenge in the territories were not to the liking of the Palestinian leftist groups. Still, they acquiesced, especially once they mended their rift with Fatah in late 1987. Matti Steinberg has attributed this attitude to the Palestinian left's perception of establishment Islam as a "safety valve in the face of fundamentalist extremism."[2] The PLO's instrumental approach to the religious revival in the territories did not go unnoticed by the Islamic Jihad, which held an uncompromising outlook that viewed jihad as a violent, unending struggle against Israel.

Still, the Islamic Jihad's rejection of the essentially secular nationalist platform of the PLO did not prevent its spokesmen from taking a pragmatic stance, incorporating strategic dogma with tactical flexibility. This approach epitomized the deep divide between the religious and nationalist camps with regard to the nature of the future Palestinian polity and the attitude toward the Arab regimes. At the same time, however, the movement held that this divide need not hinder cooperation based on tactical grounds to attain the ultimate goal: the liberation of Palestine from the yoke of occupation. Such an approach represented a sharp deviation from the immutable line adopted by the Brothers against Palestinian nationalism, by giving political legitimation to the PLO as an important, though not exclusive, force in the Palestinian scene. The pragmatic embrace of what was shared over what divided the camps was clearly reflected in an interview 'Awda gave to the East Jerusalem newspaper, *al-Fajr*, in August 1987:

> Our politico-ideological differences with the PLO do not justify the use of violence against nationalist forces. We respect the outlook of all the nationalist forces, for we believe in dialogue as the sole means of attaining mutual understanding. Our prime dispute is with the Israeli occupation.[3]

This conciliatory approach by the Islamic Jihad was aimed primarily at Fatah. In practice, it was translated into a measure of coordination and cooperation with it. The alliance between Islamic Jihad and Fatah emerged soon after the appearance of the former as an active player. It was an operative and not a political partnership of interests, as each side hoped to use the other for its own needs. Fatah aimed at channeling religious fervor toward advancing the national cause; the Islamic Jihad displayed its desire for the material gains which Fatah offered its allies, and exhibited a positive tone regarding the Islamic background of Fatah's leaders.

An early indication of this positive tone was observable in a long article in *al-Tali'a al-Islamiyya* in August 1983, which was circulated as a booklet in the Gaza Strip.[4] The article claimed that the emergence of Fatah in the early 1950s was not the result of an organizational split, nor of an Arab interest in using the Palestinian card to advance narrow goals remote from the liberation of Palestine. Rather, it was a natural continuation of the

Islamic trend led by Hajj Amin al-Husayni, 'Izz al-Din al-Qassam and 'Abd al-Qadir al-Husayni, and constituted an Islamic response to the Brothers' failure to launch jihad for liberation. The success of Fatah in re- cruiting Palestinians to armed resistance in the name of Islam turned it into a "Palestinian entity outside its land." According to the article:

> Fatah is not only the largest of the Palestinian movements, and not only the mother of the modern armed revolution, but it is also a microcosm of the Palestinian people in its entire past and present, in its responses and its struggles, in its perceptions and its uprisings....Therefore, Fatah attracts the attention of the Palestin- ian people, regardless of their political positions.[5]

Despite the Islamic Jihad's affinity with Fatah, the movement carefully preserved its independence. Moreover, it did not hesitate to criticize Fatah for its deviation from Islam and for turning its platform into "an amal- gam of Islam, nationalism, liberalism and, finally, leftist orientation." It was this mixture that impelled Fatah to pursue a policy of barter with self-interested parties in the Palestinian and regional arena, which turned "those who previously were Muslim leaders into professional politicians, and dignitaries competing among themselves for influence and status."[6] 'Arafat himself, in his political maneuvers—as in the signing of the Jor- danian-Palestinian agreement in 1985—lost his image of brave fighter in favor of "so-called experienced diplomat," who, like other Arab rulers, "holds nothing in his hand but a pen to sign with."[7]

Criticism of Fatah, however, also contained a more positive dimension: the desire to restore Fatah's authentic Islamic essence and prevent it from being sacrificed to Arab and international intrigues designed to deflect the gun pointed at Israel. This dimension was largely retained despite the deep fissure between the Islamic Jihad and Fatah engendered by the Intifada and by 'Arafat's conciliatory line over a political settlement with Israel. Signs of the fracture began to appear in the second half of 1987, which witnessed a rise in Islamic activity aimed at Israel and evoked a strong sympathetic response in the Palestinian street.

Important figures in the territories, identified with the PLO, admitted that the emergence of radical Islam reflected popular frustration with the PLO's helplessness in putting an end to the occupation.[8] However, the

Fatah leadership, domiciled in Tunis, refused to acknowledge the independent existence of such a trend. Fatah depicted it as one of the ideological streams operating within the PLO, since the organization was pluralistic and lacked any religio-ethnic base. In 'Arafat's words, "the religious trend is an integral part of the PLO, which includes the communist, the Ba'thi, the Muslim, the radical and the moderate. That is the meaning of democracy in the Palestinian revolution."[9] As proof, Fatah cited the fact that the 18th PNC conference, held in Amman, resolved to allocate seats in some PLO bodies to delegates of the religious wing in the territories. However, the only figures mentioned in this connection were 'Abd al-Rahman al-Hourani and 'Abdallah Abu 'Azah of the Gaza Strip, who were nominated as members of the PNC and the Central Council of the PLO.[10] Moreover, PLO publications identified jihad with the national Palestinian struggle, citing it as the current stage in the prolonged resistance to the occupation. Salah Halaf (Abu Iyyad), just prior to the Intifada, noted that the religious revival that swept over the territories in the 1980s was inspired by the revolutionary model embodied in Fatah, which faithfully applied the slogan of Islam: "Jihad for Allah."

> The beginning of the Islamic awakening [in the territories] lay in sanctified jihad, which was started by Fatah. This revival did not take the form of a party or a group, but those who fought within Fatah represented in their struggle and in their deaths the real meaning of Islam. Therefore, we must not differentiate between Muslim or nationalist, for there is no difference between them.[11]

While emphasizing the national imprint of the Islamic Jihad and its affinity with Fatah, Abu Iyyad denounced the factionalist stance of the Brothers for advocating non-participation in the struggle against the occupation and for devoting its energies to battering the PLO. The responsibility for the troubled relationship that developed over time between Fatah and Palestinian Islam, he said, lay with the Brothers leadership, which refused to cooperate with Fatah, on the false premise that Fatah led young people to hell and not to jihad. This refusal was puzzling in light of the aid and support given to Fatah by the other branches of the Brothers in the Arab world.

Despite this sharp criticism, however, Abu Iyyad took a conciliatory approach, imploring the Brothers to respond to the PLO's appeal for unity of the ranks, as disputation only served Israel.[12] A similar attitude was expressed by another Fatah leader, Salim al-Za'anun (Abu al-Adib), who declared that "the affiliation of the Islamic trend with the Palestinian resistance will constitute a great victory for the Palestinian national struggle."[13]

The paternalism displayed by Fatah toward Palestinian Islam increased with the eruption of the Intifada. This was reflected in a denial of the important role played by Islamic Jihad in initiating the Intifada, and in attempts to assimilate it into the UNC. Fatah spokesmen attributed the public debate over the role of the Islamic trend in the uprising to the "Zionist media," which wanted thereby to achieve two goals: focus the limelight on the internal struggles of the Palestinians; and stir apprehension among Western countries so that they would acquiesce in the criminal measures taken by Israel against the popular Intifada.[14] Side by side with this paternalistic approach, Fatah began to use the Intifada as a lever for promoting political compromise with Israel. This development reached a peak at the 19th PNC conference in Algiers (November 1988), which declared an independent Palestinian state while granting de facto recognition to the legitimate existence of Israel.[15]

The decisions of the PNC conference were described by Islamic Jihad as a "severe deviation from the path of armed struggle." They elicited a more antagonistic attitude by the Islamic Jihad toward Fatah, sharpening the ideological and political differences between the two sides. This approach, besides conveying protest against an ally who had abandoned the Palestinian cause, reflected real distress within the Islamic Jihad, which in the early months of the Intifada found itself trailing behind both the UNC and Hamas, a situation exacerbated by the exile of its leaders in Lebanon. The change in its attitude toward the PLO dovetailed to a great extent with the stance of its patron, Iran. At the start of the Islamic Revolution, Iran had close ties with the PLO, but it gradually grew more hostile toward the organization in the wake of the neutral, and later pro-Iraqi line adopted by 'Arafat during the Iran-Iraq War; his close ties with the "reactionary" Gulf states; and his efforts to reach a political settlement with Israel.[16]

Reacting to the PNC decisions, the Islamic Jihad published a manifesto accusing the members of the PNC of ignorance in their grasp of the essence of the struggle with the Jews over Palestine:

> You are forging your path today over the bodies of your remnants and your brothers, crossing the sanctified sea of blood in order to shake hands with those who kill you and steal your lands; to raise a toast to a contaminated peace; and to divide the homeland, the homeland of faith.[17]

The manifesto pronounced the submissive decisions adopted by the 19th PNC conference under pressure from Arab and Western states as null and void. This was so both because it ignored the Islamic trend's position, which represented an important segment of the Palestinian people, and because of the legal prohibition against dividing up "the homeland with the enemy." Therefore, the movement declared, it would carry on with jihad against the occupation, since this expressed the will of Allah and was the only guarantee of an ultimate Muslim victory over the forces of apostasy in the region.[18] Biting criticism of Fatah's intensive search for a political settlement and of its distancing itself from Islam, was a recurrent theme in the movement's statements. The Palestinian problem, Shiqaqi and 'Awda pointed out, was a pure Islamic issue that concerned all Muslims and not the Palestinians alone. They warned that excluding Islam from the battlefield in Palestine would inevitably lead to heightened friction among the Palestinian political forces and to a break between the people and their leadership.[19]

The movement rejected 'Arafat's view that in the "new world order" created in the aftermath of the Cold War and the Gulf War, a more realistic approach to a settlement with Israel must be taken in order to advance Palestinian interests. In the movement's view, the perception that absolute justice ('adl mutlaq) must be abandoned in favor of obtainable justice ('adl mumkin) was mistaken. The movement argued that the international balance of power remained as it had been at the start of the 20th century, still tilting toward Israel, despite the upheavals in Eastern Europe and the collapse of the Soviet Union. The US, having supplanted Britain as the policeman of the Middle East, sought to mold the region according to its premises and interests, namely, by strengthening Israel and keeping the Palestinian problem marginal.[20] Therefore, any peace agreement to settle the conflict in the region was nothing but an agreement of submission, in which the strong side (Israel) imposed its will on the other side (the Arab states and the PLO), which lacked any military option. The dangers hidden in this kind of peace agreement did not end with the granting of legal legitimation to Israel's existence and the dispossession of the Palestinians, but also included turning the capitals of the Arab states into the prime focus of Zionist intrigue.[21]

The shift in Fatah's stance, which positioned the tactical line (the phased plan) as a declared alternative to the strategic line (the full liberation of Palestine), evoked the outbreak of the Intifada, a response to the search for peaceful solutions. In revolting against the occupation, 'Awda noted, the Palestinians made it clear that their struggle was not for boundaries (*sira' hudud*) but for existence (*sira' wujud*), engendered by the expulsion of one side by the other.[22] Palestine needed a credible leadership, rather than power-seekers who abandon the path of revolution in order to barter with the blood of martyrs for the advancement of personal interests. The antithesis of the PLO's false leadership, in the Islamic Jihad's view, was Nelson Mandela, leader of the blacks in South Africa, who chose imprisonment for 27 years over freedom that was offered to him in exchange for denouncing violent acts against the white minority's repressive regime. As a consequence of his patience and tenacity, South Africa was restored to its lawful masters and he himself became its president.[23]

Along with this harsh criticism, the Islamic Jihad denied the existence of any operational connection with Fatah. This combination of criticism and denial had a practical motive—the movement's desire to reaffirm its political independence and to reestablish itself in the religious camp, whose main exponent, Hamas, had become the leading Islamic force in the Intifada. This was well reflected in the dissemination by the Islamic Jihad of independent leaflets and its decision to remain outside the UNC, as well as its display of reservations toward other Jihad factions linked to Fatah. Shiqaqi termed these groups ephemeral and marginal, claiming that they did not represent the true concept of jihad in Palestine, which existed in its most coherent form in the Islamic Jihad.[24] Two groups in particular were singled out for discredit: the Islamic Jihad Squads (*Sarayat al-Jihad al-Islami*), and the Islamic Jihad-Jerusalem (*al-Jihad al-Islami Bayt al-Maqdis*).

Shiqaqi admitted that his movement had maintained an operational link with the Islamic Jihad Squads during the period prior to the Intifada, based on an understanding that this coordination would enhance military activity against the occupation. However, following the death in Limassol of the Squads' three commanders (February 1988), that faction retreated from its commitment to Islam and became strongly identified with Fatah, prompting the Islamic Jihad to cut off ties with it.[25] The other Jihad faction, the Islamic Jihad-Jerusalem, based in Jordan, and headed by Shaykh As'ad Bayyud al-Tamimi, was accused by the Islamic Jihad of serving as a tool of Fatah to foment factionalism in the Islamic camp in order to gain support for its concessions to Israel. The Islamic Jihad denounced Tamimi for his close ties with 'Arafat, who had appointed his son Nadir as mufti of the Palestinian Liberation Army; for taking part in the PNC's 20th conference in Algiers (September 1991), which ratified the participation of a Palestinian delegation in the peace talks with Israel; and for distancing himself from Iran following the Kuwait crisis and siding with Saddam Husayn, whom he had called "the second Salah al-Din."[26] Underlying these sharp accusations was the Islamic Jihad's desire to establish itself as the key force in the emergence of radical Islam in Palestine, as well as to stain Tamimi's image with Iran, which had granted him financial and logistic support.

Rejecting these accusations, Tamimi claimed that it was he who had founded the Islamic Jihad in 1980, following which such key activists as Shiqaqi, Ahmad Muhanna and Ibrahim Sarbal left and established competing factions. In 1989 he had added the name "Jerusalem" to his movement, which, he explained, was the "promised home of the Islamic caliphate." Tamimi thus presented his group as the other component of the Islamic equation in Palestine, alongside Hamas, while also taking credit for all the jihad military acts perpetrated against Israel before the Intifada.[27] At the same time, he sought to undermine Shiqaqi's credibility, portraying him as indecisive and as having been expelled from the Islamic Jihad in the early 1980s for treachery based on illicit contacts with various elements in the Arab world. Justifying his support for Iraq during the Gulf crisis, Tamimi argued that the campaign against "crusaders" took precedence over all else, and that, moreover, Kuwait was a part of Iraq. Saddam Husayn had the right, even the duty, to annex it in order to unify the nation toward the goal of liberating Palestine. He rejected the accusation that by siding with the Iraqi ruler he had distanced Iran, his traditional ally. "There is no personal animosity between me and Saddam Husayn, just as there is no familial relationship between me and the Iranians," he said.[28]

On the question of his ties with Fatah, Tamimi argued that they were permissible according to the Shari'a, and said they would be maintained so long as Fatah did not deny Islam or its principles, especially the duty of jihad. Moreover, his movement's consent to fill six seats in PLO bodies—three in the PNC and three in the Central Council—and his son Nadr's readiness to serve as mufti of the Palestinian Liberation Army, were designed to permit a more effective struggle against Fatah's political line.[29]

Tamimi's stance, which favored opposition activity within the PLO rather than outside it, conflicted with that of the Islamic Jihad, which rejected out of hand any possibility of joining the PLO or even the PNC. According to al-Mujahid, the PNC had become an unrepresentative vehicle ever since the mid-1980s, its debates serving only as a decorative cover for endorsing the submissive policy of Fatah. Not only would the integration of the Islamic Jihad into the PNC amount to a denial of its central principle (the unity of the armed struggle takes priority over the unity of the organization); it would also damage its credibility in the eyes of the Palestinians, who insist on an Islamic solution to their distress.[30] Lashing out at Tamimi, Shiqaqi charged that a true Muslim must reject any participation in the "funeral procession of Palestine" that 'Arafat leads.[31] The only way to coalesce a united front of national and religious camps, he said, was through a substantive reform of the PLO platform and its bodies so as to renew the commitment to Islam and armed struggle.[32]

Still, despite their aversion to the PLO's political line and their refusal to join its institutions, Islamic Jihad leaders declared that they harbored no hostility toward it and did not view themselves as an alternative leadership. Their movement never opposed the PLO's role as an umbrella framework for the Palestinian forces. Yet, it was their right and duty to provide an alternative platform in Islamic terms, to replace the ideological anarchy of retreat and deviation.[33] The struggle with the PLO over the image of Palestinian society, however, would be determined democratically, after routing the occupation and establishing a state in all of Palestine.[34]

The Islamic Jihad drew a distinction between the PLO as a patriotic framework (*itar watani*) that merited support in light of its sustained resistance to the occupation, and the PLO as a political trend (*tawajjuh siyasi*), which was rejected on religious and moral grounds. Accordingly, crises that occurred in the PLO—such as the tarnishing of its Arab and international status for supporting Iraq during the Gulf War—did not constitute a breakdown for the Palestinians, but merely a crisis for 'Arafat and his concessionary policy.[35] This distinction, shared to a large extent by Hamas as well, reflected a realistic desire by political Islam to avoid denouncing the PLO publicly, so as not to harm its chances of widening the base of its support among the Palestinians. Fatah, by contrast, rejected this distinction, viewing it as a delegitimation of the PLO and a challenge to its unique status as the sole representative of the Palestinian people. In a polemical article in *Filastin al-Thawra* (July 1990) that was essentially critical of Hamas, Fatah asserted:

> Every deviation or attempt to deviate from the traditions and regulations of this house [i.e., the PLO] fall into the category of apostasy....The house of the PLO is the house of the homeland and the Palestinian entity, and therefore any rivalry with it is a rivalry with the homeland. The PLO is the state and not a party within the state. This is a fact that many apostates ignore.[36]

Sharper criticism was voiced by the nationalist poet Mahmud Darwish, who accused the Islamic trend of serving Israel's interests by politicizing religion and opposing the call for peaceful coexistence between Arabs and Jews. He branded the leaders of Islamic Jihad and Hamas "terrorists" who threaten democracy, which they perceive as granted to them but forbidden to others. Responding, the Islamic Jihad argued that the Jews never preached coexistence with the Arabs; moreover, they view Palestinians who do not belong to the Islamic trend as terrorists, too. Darwish's main fear, shared by the PLO elite, was the revolutionary message that preached jihad until victory or martyrdom.[37]

Fatah's blunt attack on Palestinian Islam marked a sharp retreat from its tactic of patronage in the wake of the Intifada, reflecting its awareness that the Islamic trend, and especially Hamas, constituted a palpable threat to the status of the PLO. The troubled relationship with Fatah was also

reflected in the Islamic Jihad's operative attitude to the UNC.[38] The movement's refusal to join the UNC because of its strong affinity with the PLO
and its misuse of financial resources, diminished the coordination that
had existed between the two sides at the start of the Intifada regarding
strikes and demonstrations. This refusal, in turn, enhanced mutual re-
criminations,[39] although without deteriorating into violence (unlike
clashes that broke out between Fatah and Hamas activists in the territories at the time). The Islamic Jihad continued to maintain its declared
tactical position, namely that ideological and political disputes must not
interfere with the unity of the struggle against the occupation.

By the start of 1990, however, the focus of Islamic Jihad had shifted
from Fatah to the Palestinian left, which, despite its anti-religious outlook, remained loyal to the strategy of popular armed resistance. In contrast to Fatah, which granted Islam a place of honor, the Palestinian left
espoused a quasi-atheistic approach that excluded religion from the public
domain, treating it solely as a belief system between man and his creator.
In its writings, the Palestinian left portrayed its Marxist world view as
progressive and enlightened, constituting an antithesis to the antiquated
outlook of the "reactionary" camp in the Arab world, which also included
the Islamic movements. However, it refrained from open opposition to
Islam and chose to ignore the issue of the role of Islam in Palestinian society, so as not to jeopardize its popular base of support. This pragmatic
view reflected an internal dilemma in the Palestinian left, which was further complicated by the collapse of communism in Europe and the religious revival in the territories in the 1980s.[40]

The religious revival in the territories pushed the Palestinian left onto
the defensive, forcing it to break its thundering silence over Islam and
recognize it as an important cultural component in molding Palestinian
identity. Prior to and during the early months of the Intifada, Palestinian
leftist spokesmen acknowledged the growing influence of Islam in the
territories, although they placed it in the broader "objective" context of a
religious revival in the Arab world generally. The causes of this broad
development, they argued, were the failure of the "bourgeois" Arab regimes to solve socioeconomic problems in their countries, and the dual
influence of the Islamic Revolution in Iran and the Islamic resistance in
Lebanon.[41] Recognizing the growing power of Palestinian Islam, the leftist factions adopted a two-pronged approach:

1. Denouncing the traditional Islamic trend embodied in the Brothers for preaching sectarianism and for serving as a tool of Israel and the "reactionary" Arab states (especially Saudi Arabia and Jordan) to destroy Palestinian unity. This condemnation echoed the *Mujamma'* campaign of incitement to violence against leftist circles in the Gaza Strip, who were portrayed as linked to "heresy, apostasy and communism."

2. Adopting a positive tone toward the revolutionary Islamic trend, embodied by the Islamic Jihad, for its nationalist coloration and its drive to repress ideological disagreements with the Palestinian nationalist camp in favor of the uncompromising struggle against Israel.[42]

Commending Islamic Jihad, however, did not inhibit the Palestinian left from criticizing the movement's decision to stay out of the UNC and to circulate its own leaflets. Leftist figures stated that cooperation with the PLO without participating in its institutions was evidence that the Islamic Jihad had not entirely dissociated itself from its progenitor, the Brothers. In fact, its real aim was to accumulate achievements so as to compete more effectively with the national democratic trend.[43]

Fearing political marginalization, the Palestinian left made efforts to blunt the religious challenge. Its leaders spurred Fatah to act in two spheres: tightening its ties with the Islamic Jihad so as to highlight the latter's nationalist content, and renewing the armed struggle. According to PFLP leader George Habash, the ability of the PLO to halt the drift to religion by Palestinian youth depended entirely on the ratification of its loyalty to armed struggle. "The Palestinian public, which wants the liberation of Palestine...will back the force that it believes can continue the struggle to attain this goal," Habash said.[44]

Habash's appeal for the renewal of armed confrontation, however, went unanswered in light of the "peace assault" mounted by Fatah and its use of the Intifada as a tactical maneuver to attain diplomatic gains. This development sharpened the traditional tension between the Palestinian left and Fatah over shaping PLO policy, a struggle exacerbated by a mini-conflict within the UNC over the nature of the Intifada. The leftist components of the UNC, led by the PFLP, were sharply critical of the policy of restraint adopted by the Command and accused it of failing to advance the Intifada to the stage of a "general national revolt."[45] The internal rifts in the PLO over the issue of armed struggle, together with a mounting demand by the DFLP and PFLP for reforms in the PLO bodies in order to break Fatah's monopoly in them, laid the groundwork for a tactical alliance between the Palestinian left and the Islamic Jihad.

The Islamic Jihad did not conceal its view that ever since the 1950s, the secular platform of the Palestinian left had sought to abolish the role of Islam both in society and in the field of battle against Israel. This agenda was portrayed by the movement as "the continuation of the Western cultural invasion, which has grasped our nation in its claws." Spokesmen for the movement noted that the Palestinian left in effect had cooperated in the submissive resolutions made at the 19th PNC conference, by virtue of its wavering stance during the debates. Nevertheless, the Islamic Jihad welcomed the left's readiness to cooperate with Palestinian Islam in the framework of the Intifada.[46] It also expressed hope that the bankruptcy of communism would prompt the Palestinian left to recognize its error and adopt Islam as the sole means for the liberation of Palestine.[47] The movement's positive tone was aimed primarily at Habash's organization, and was put into practice with the circulation of joint leaflets in the territories and the refugee camps in Lebanon, as well as a joint presence at Arab conferences on the Intifada.[48]

The Islamic Jihad also cultivated close ties with the pro-Syrian Palestinian factions outside the PLO framework, especially the PFLP-GC led by Ahmad Jibril. Clearly, the background for this convergence was Jibril's supportive attitude toward Iran and his ties with it.[49] In contrast to the PLO's reserved position, Jibril announced his unequivocal support for the Iranian revolution as an important element of the strategy for the liberation of Palestine. Quoting Khomeini in depicting Israel as "a cancerous growth that must be uprooted," he advocated infusing the Palestinian problem with a broad regional dimension so that it not remain caged in a narrow local context. In acknowledging the power of Palestinian Islam, Jibril stated that he did not accept the distinction between political and spiritual Islam, claiming that Islamic identity serves as an important tool in advancing the goal of the liberation of Palestine.[50]

Although the Islamic Jihad sided with the demand of the Palestinian left for reforms in the PLO institutions, it rejected its demand that one of the conditions for such change was the co-option of the Islamic trend into the PLO in order to heighten internal pressure for reform.[51] According to the movement's organ, al-Mujahid, the PLO bodies lacked any affinity for democracy. Moreover, the chances for reform were significantly diminished by the dominance of Fatah and its determination to keep the Islamic movement out of the PLO by posing unacceptable conditions for its entry. The primary effort should be focused on the territories, for "the freedom of the Palestinian will not be determined from outside."[52]

The Islamic Jihad's reservations about taking part in PLO institutions reflected ideological cleavages that were being repressed for the moment. Nevertheless, the movement was prepared to advance the unity of the struggle with the Palestinian left.[53] Various spokesmen from both sides confirmed that in addition to local coordination, an intensive dialogue was being conducted to consolidate a broader operative alliance.[54] The urgency of such a development was explained by Shaykh Sayyid Baraka, one of the Islamic Jihad leaders who had been expelled to Lebanon in January 1989: "The role of the revolutionaries is to save all that is holy and to guard it, and not to renounce or abandon it regardless of differences of opinion. The right of dispute is sanctified in Islam."[55]

Islamic Jihad-Brothers/Hamas Relations

Relations between the Islamic Jihad and the Brothers were characterized by a dogmatic consensus (over the notion of an Islamic state in Palestine) side by side with a tactical dispute (on methods of implementation). As has been shown, the Islamic Jihad emerged from the ranks of *al-Mujama'* in the Gaza Strip, positing itself as an antithesis to the Brothers. The Islamic Jihad's criticism of the Brothers focused on three central issues: the Palestinian problem, the Islamic Revolution in Iran, and the Arab regimes.

1. The Palestinian problem. The Brothers deviated from Hasan al-Banna's legacy and from his commitment to Palestine. They adopted a gradualist approach, which ignored the unique position of Palestine, and a mode of operation suited to other arenas in the Middle East. This mistaken approach treated the Palestinian problem merely as another Islamic issue, its resolution conditional upon completing the processes of reform in Muslim society and the establishment of an Islamic state outside Palestine. Once established, this Islamic state would hoist the banner of jihad and would act to liberate all Islamic lands under foreign occupation, including that of Palestine. In Shiqaqi's view, the perception of Palestine as a secondary element in a larger overall program ignored the centrality of

Palestine in the struggle against the forces of evil. The fact that a large Islamic state under a caliph or imam had not yet been established was no reason for postponing jihad in Palestine. On the contrary, the greater the progress of jihad in Palestine, the more power Islam would acquire.[56]

Furthermore, the Brothers' focus on the social aspect of Islam narrowed its true meaning as a comprehensive ideology that recognized no separation between religion and politics, and no neglect of the duty of jihad. Armed jihad against an infidel regime, the Islamic Jihad argued, served as a complementary component and not a hindrance to communal activity. Its absence could lead only to the dissolution of society, turning it into easy prey for its enemies. Authentic Islam, therefore, is that which conducts a constant dialogue with the surrounding reality and faithfully expresses the aspirations of the Palestinians.[57] Another aspect determined by the Brothers' stagnant outlook regarding Palestine was their alienated attitude toward the PLO. In Shiqaqi's view, since priority must be given to direct confrontation with the occupation, there was no religious or moral justification for the attacks conducted by the Brothers against national groups, which only served the enemy. "The Qur'an commands us to cooperate with the pure and the faithful and not with the debased and the conqueror."[58]

2. The Islamic Revolution in Iran. The Brothers failed to understand the sharp change that the Islamic Revolution had brought about in the status of Islam and in its relationship with its enemies. In the wake of the Iran-Iraq War, and under pressure from their progenitors in Egypt and Jordan, the Brothers in Palestine retreated from their initial sympathetic stand regarding the Islamic Revolution. Together with 'ulama', they strove to widen the theological gaps between Sunna and Shi'a as a precondition for inflaming hostility among the Palestinians toward the followers of Khomeini—Islamic Jihad members, who were denounced as "Shi'is." Looking back, Shiqaqi wrote, the accusation of Shi'ism was an evil plot to deflect attention from the need for armed jihad to liberate Palestine. The Islamic Jihad's position toward Shi'a did not deviate from that of the Sunni legal sages. The Brothers' charge that the Islamic Revolution had strayed from its Islamic principles was baseless, for the unification of the Muslim nation is its chief aim.[59]

3. The Arab governments. Hostility toward the Islamic Revolution was increasingly unjustifiable, the Islamic Jihad argued, in light of the

Brothers' advocacy of coexistence with the Arab governments despite the fact that these regimes maintained close ties with Western imperialism. The Arab regimes, and especially Egypt, Jordan and Saudi Arabia, served as a "security belt around Israel" and "believe in the satans of Washington rather than in Allah." Reconciliation with them was further evidence of the Brothers' detachment from the historic context, which requires a war to the end against those very regimes, for their impotence and hostility toward Islam.[60]

The Brothers, responding to these grave accusations, noted their beneficial activity in Palestine long before, and during, the Israeli occupation. They emphasized the multi-faceted nature of jihad, and the need to carry it out in stages. "The entire life of the Muslim is a chain of jihad, consisting of all types of jihad," stated a leader of the Brothers in the West Bank.[61]

The Brothers anchored their alienation from the PLO in the religious injunction against any tie or affinity with groups that exclude Islam from their ideological platform, whatever their contribution to Palestine.[62] An even more radical undertone, aimed at the PLO's left wing, was discernible in remarks by Subhi 'Anabtawi, a prominent Nablus merchant and high-ranking leader of the Brothers. The real enemies of Islam at the present time, he said, were not the Jews but leftist leaders of the Palestinian revolution, who were heretics and did not live by the Shari'a.[63] The Islamic Jihad's focus on the political aspect of Islam and its relations with the PLO angered the Brothers, who viewed this as an absence of ideological backbone and a useful tool for 'Arafat.

Viewed retrospectively, the ideological and political dispute that divided the Islamic Jihad from the Brothers precluded any possibility of compromise or convergence. Ultimately, it led to the rise of a bitter rivalry involving periodic violent confrontations. A main venue for these clashes was the Islamic University campus—e.g., the attack there in 1983 upon 'Awda, then a lecturer at the university, by Brothers members; and clashes between the two sides in late 1987, when Islamic Jihad sympathizers demonstrated against the Israeli decision to expel 'Awda. In 'Awda's view, the Brothers' campaign against his movement since its appearance on the Palestinian scene hindered the Islamic Jihad's efforts to mount a struggle against Israel sooner.[64]

A new chapter in the relations between the two movements began on the eve of the Intifada, with the establishment of Hamas as an activist arm of the Brothers in the Gaza Strip. According to Steinberg, "The Brothers required a historical catalyst in the form of the Intifada before they...abandoned the road of restraint that had, so far, characterized *al-Mujamma'*."[65] The creation of Hamas served to neutralize intergenerational tensions in the Brothers' ranks, while also counteracting the political challenge posed by the Islamic Jihad.[66]

The Islamic Jihad's military activity, which elicited growing support among the Palestinians, alongside friction within the Brothers, resulted in a difficult dilemma for the Brothers leadership. On the one hand, they feared that holding back from direct confrontation with the occupation would lead to a drift of supporters to the Islamic Jihad, and a loss of the ability to take part in decisive political processes in the Palestinian arena. On the other hand, there was a pronounced desire not to stray significantly from the conservative stance regarding Palestine, so as not to blur the distinctive features of the Brothers. The solution was the formation of Hamas, which constituted a compromise: integration into the Intifada and the struggle against Israel, while preserving the ideological and organizational framework of the Brothers.[67] Moreover, the fact that the operative arena of Hamas largely overlapped the geographical boundaries of Palestine reflected the growing Palestinian identity of the Brothers and their determined effort to influence the course of the Intifada.

Hamas' affinity to its parent movement, the Brothers, was demonstrated on two levels:

1. Ideologically, Hamas stressed that even though it was a new factor on the Palestinian stage, it was the product of a long historic process. It was heir to the Islamic movements, headed by the Brothers, that held the Qur'an in one hand and a gun in the other.[68] Paragraph 2 of its charter (August 1988) explicitly stated that "Hamas is one of the wings of the Muslim Brothers in Palestine," which is a world movement.[69] By contrast, Hamas belittled the role of the Islamic Jihad, holding that the Intifada broke out as a result of a chain of successful attacks carried out by "Muslim youths" in the territories during 1987.[70]

2. Politically, Hamas sharpened the Brothers' dispute with the PLO over the issue of political settlement. It also widened the venue of the rivalry from the campus and local centers of power to the Palestinian street.[71]

The emergence of Hamas as the leading Islamic force in the Intifada, combined with the intensified PLO effort to seek a political compromise with Israel, put the Islamic Jihad on the defensive and prompted it to adopt a conciliatory approach to the "big sister," Hamas. This approach emphasized the need to form a united Islamic front against the occupation and the PLO's political maneuvers, and to promote the Intifada until the banner of jihad was hoisted over the land of Palestine.[72]

Addressing Hamas, the Islamic Jihad had stressed the centrality of Islamic unity to its movement long before the Intifada, even when the ideological gap between it and the Brothers was wide. According to Shiqaqi, allowing this unity to remain in the realm of rhetoric without fleshing it out with substantive content amounted to the violation of a religious obligation. The quest for Islamic unity, however, did not mean discarding a particular ideological line, or ignoring the right of others to pledge loyalty to a specific group and leadership. Each party was entitled to preserve its independent existence, so long as it remained within the confines of cooperation against the occupation, i.e., promoting unity while preserving distinctiveness. The greater the consensus over the Palestinian issue, the greater the chances of minimizing disputes over other issues, such as the PLO or the Iranian revolution.[73] 'Awda, approaching Hamas, declared:

> It is our duty to understand that Muslims complement each other. The Islamic Jihad's perception does not push aside any other. Rather, it emerged during the competition over what is good, and in order to fill a large vacuum that had brought suffering in the Palestinian and Islamic arenas....Thus, the Islamic Jihad complements Hamas, and the opposite is called for.[74]

Not only must armed struggle against the occupation be the highest priority of the Islamic groups, the Islamic Jihad urged, but it must also be central in their relationship with the secular forces operating in Palestine. Moreover, along with attaining understanding over the conduct of the struggle, the contentious ideological and political issues must be clarified. This must be accomplished by dialogue, not confrontation. Otherwise, the efforts at coordinating the main campaign would be foiled and the confusion of the Palestinian masses would mount.[75]

The Islamic Jihad thus voiced its dismay with the ongoing internal strife in the Palestinian arena, which thwarted the popular, surging nature of the Intifada. Reacting to the growing power struggle between Fatah and Hamas in the territories, the movement, while accepting the existence of several political trends, insisted that unity in the struggle against the enemy should take priority over party interests.[76] Yet, the movement's basic premise that Islam was the sole vehicle for self-identity and for struggle weakened its claim of recognition of Palestinian political pluralism.[77]

Hamas, for its part, also declared its commitment to furthering harmony within Palestinian Islam, viewing the multiplicity of groupings as a "natural" phenomenon, by virtue of the sanctified principle of *ijtihad* (human endeavor) in Islam. Hamas, however, emphasized its distinctiveness as a deep-rooted Islamic movement in Palestinian society, with regional backing, claiming that it alone had the power to bring about "the complete liberation of Palestine and the establishment of the rule of Allah."[78] It also pointed to the extensive fragmentation within Palestinian Islamic Jihad, as well as to the location of its entire leadership outside the territories, as causes of the movement's limited activity in the Intifada.[79] This elitist perception lay at the center of Hamas' refusal to move beyond narrow local coordination with the Islamic Jihad in the Intifada. Hamas' exclusiveness, however, was cloaked in a practical explanation: the absence of a climate conducive to convergence between the various Islamic forces because of the necessity to function clandestinely. The security factor was also used by Hamas as a further explanation for refusing to take part in the UNC, which, it claimed, was "a framework that was easy for Israeli intelligence to penetrate."[80]

Regarding its troubled relationship with the PLO, Hamas insisted that it did not view itself as an alternative to the PLO. Hamas acknowledged the PLO's many years of efforts to preserve Palestinian identity and foster the evolution of the Palestinians from a nation of refugees to one capable of rising up against its oppressor. However, in contrast to the Islamic Jihad, it held that the issue of cooperation with the PLO could not be limited to the sphere of opposition to the occupation, but constituted a political and moral issue. Hamas, known for its commitment to the principle of denying Israel any legal rights in Palestine, could not be untrue to itself and operate on the same front as the PLO, which was prepared to make far-reaching territorial concessions.[81]

Like the Islamic Jihad, Hamas made a distinction between the PLO as a recognized patriotic framework and the PLO's political line, which it rejected out of hand. However, unlike the Islamic Jihad, whose criticism of the PLO focused on the issue of armed struggle, Hamas vigorously sought to undermine and replace the PLO's political primacy in the territories. In this context, the publication of the Hamas charter in 1988 served a double function: it provided an ideological basis for the justification of the movement's independent existence and presented a political alternative to the PLO on the issue of the conflict with Israel. Articulating the distinctiveness of Hamas, Paragraph 6 of the charter stated that "its loyalty is to Allah and Islam as a way of life, and its goal is to raise the banner of Allah over every inch of Palestine." Elsewhere it emphasized Hamas' "role of guarding the continued existence of the PLO as a framework for activity, yet not preventing people from expressing their support for and loyalty to Hamas and its jihad platform."[82]

The issue of the relationship with the PLO, although in dispute, did not limit the range of cooperative relations between the two Islamic movements, which became more practical in view of the need to block 'Arafat's "journey of political submissiveness." As reported in November 1990, in a series of secret contacts between Hamas representatives based in Saudi Arabia and the Islamic Jihad's leaders, the two sides considered a joint program for strengthening the Palestinian Islamic camp vis-à-vis the PLO.[83] This declared goal was not achieved, but the talks laid the foundations for closer coordination regarding the Intifada (joint communiques, strikes and trade union election strategies). Such contacts became more intensive in the wake of the Gulf crisis.[84] Iran and the Muslim Brothers in Jordan played a key role in efforts at mediation.

In June 1990 and February 1991, joint Jordanian Brothers-Hamas delegations traveled to Tehran to discuss the state of the Intifada, as well as "American aggression" in the Gulf crisis, with the Iranian leadership. The Iranians, anxious to advance their standing in the Sunni world and to gain a foothold in Palestinian politics, announced their complete support for the Intifada and the liberation of Palestine.[85] Nevertheless, Hamas adopted a cautious line in its contacts with Iran, for two main reasons. The first pertained to the Brothers' ideological stance regarding the Islamic Revolution and its Shi'ite coloring. According to *Filastin al-Muslima* (the Hamas organ published in London), the Islamic Revolution had played no direct role in the emergence of the Islamic activist trend in the Middle East. It was, however, "a strong expression of the start of a new era of Islamic resurgence created by the 'ulama' and thinkers during decades of activity, forbearance and jihad."[86] The second reason was pragmatic, namely, Hamas' desire to avoid damaging its cordial relations with its benefactors, the Gulf states and Jordan, sworn rivals of Iran.[87] Confirmation of this was provided by Hamas' stand regarding the Iraqi takeover of Kuwait in August 1990. The movement opposed the Iraqi invasion, viewing it as a crude violation of the sovereignty of a neighboring Arab state. Later, however, it took a firm position against the entry of Western forces into the Gulf region.

The Islamic Jihad, too, opposed the occupation of Kuwait, but on the grounds of abhorring the slaughter of Muslims—which served only Israel and marginalized the Palestinian issue—rather than in support of Kuwaiti independence. The movement denounced the Gulf regimes as heretical and repeatedly pointed to Iran as the only country able to resolve the Palestinian issue through armed jihad. Hamas, for its part, while praising Iran for its preparedness to assist in solving the crisis by peaceful means, continued to view the Arab states as its main benefactors. Such differences in viewpoint between Hamas and the Islamic Jihad, however, did not prevent either of them from making political capital out of the PLO's defensive position as a result of its siding with Saddam Husayn.[88]

The convergence between Hamas, the Islamic Jihad and Iran, however tentative, and the political dynamics in the region created by the Madrid peace conference (October 1991), spurred a new array of relationships on the Palestinian scene, namely a coalition of the Palestinian religious and rejectionist camps against Fatah. An important milestone in the dialogue between these two camps was marked at a conference in Damascus (January 1992) in which delegates of the Islamic Jihad and Hamas participated along with representatives of the opposition groups within the PLO and outside it. A concluding joint communique stated that the bilateral and multilateral peace talks with Israel violated the historic rights of the Palestinians. The participants, the communique continued, committed themselves to mutual cooperation for the advancement of the Intifada and firmer resistance to Fatah's political line.[89] This announcement was followed by the establishment in September 1992 of the Ten Palestinian Factions, comprising among its members the Islamic Jihad, Hamas, al-

Sa'iqa, PFLP, DFLP-GC, DFLP (Democratic Front for the Liberation of Palestine) and the PRCP (Palestinian Revolutionary Communist Party).[90]

Cooperation between the religious and other anti-Fatah factions, which remained essentially on the political level, marked a victory for the Islamic Jihad approach, which underscored the common grounds (armed struggle) over divisive factors (the role of religion in Palestinian society). However, while the rejectionist camp viewed cooperation as a means to erode Fatah power, Hamas saw it as a means to undermine the PLO's status. Accordingly, Hamas leaders demanded the establishment of an authoritative forum to coordinate the opposition, with Hamas' representation to be commensurate with its elevated position in the territories.[91] These conflicting aims were aptly described by George Habash in an interview with *Filastin al-Muslima* in December 1991:

> Coordination is one thing and the establishment of fronts is another. At the present stage, we cannot think of establishing a front, but rather of acting to attain the highest degree of cooperation. It is important to emphasize that all thoughts of establishing a front in the future, as circumstances dictate, must be realized on the basis of preserving the existence of the PLO and rectifying its political line, and under no circumstances constituting a replacement for it.[92]

Since Habash's statement in 1991, the Palestinian arena had undergone a series of upheavals, including the waning of the Intifada and the advance of the peace process, which reached a climax with the Oslo Accords (1993) and the setting up of the Palestinian Authority (PA; 1994). To what extent had the Islamic Jihad and Hamas remained loyal to their ideological platform? To what extent had ideological dogma regarding the nature of the struggle and the role of Islam in society given way to political flexibility in a changing environment? These questions will be addressed in the chapter that follows.

Chapter Four:
The Oslo Accords—Ideology and Political Reality

The cornerstone of Islamic Jihad's ideology was the belief that Palestine was the focal point of the historio-cultural struggle between the Muslims and their eternal enemies, the Jews and the Christians. The liberation of Palestine by a holy war was a prerequisite for the unification of the Muslims and the restoration of Islamic superiority. In presenting the conflict over Palestine as an existential struggle for the Muslims, the Islamic Jihad sought to attain two objectives: (1) Reemphasizing the Islamic essence of the conflict with Israel; and (2) Placing itself as the spearhead of the struggle over Palestine, thereby gaining recognition as a vital factor in Palestinian politics meriting support both domestically and abroad.

The sanctification of Palestine determined the Islamic Jihad's negative stance toward the peace process as well. The movement's narrative left no doubt about its view of Palestine as *waqf* land, which no one had the right to barter away. Adhering to this premise, the movement condemned the PLO's abandonment of the strategy of complete liberation of Palestine in favor of a historic compromise with Israel. The Islamic Jihad also continued to repel various feelers by representatives of 'Arafat, such as Executive Committee members Nasir Yusuf and 'Abbas Zaki, regarding the possibility of joining PLO bodies.[1] 'Arafat vented his frustration over this rejection by denouncing Islamic Jihad as an agent of Shi'ite Iran, whose goal was to sow divisiveness among Palestinians. In response, the movement charged that 'Arafat's attacks were meant to guarantee the survival of the PLO on behalf of his patrons—the West and the Arab regimes—in their fight against the Islamic trend. His accusations against the Islamic Jihad, Shiqaqi claimed, essentially reflected contempt for the stamina of the Palestinian people and their ability to defend themselves on their own.[2]

In seeking a political solution to the Palestinian problem, the PLO was motivated not only by its need to deal with the changing global situation following the collapse of the Eastern Bloc. It was also guided by the desire to extricate itself from its political isolation, the result of supporting the Iraqi ruler in the Gulf War (1991), and to establish its seniority in the territories against the political challenge embodied by Palestinian Islam.

Signing the Oslo Accords on the White House lawn (September 1993) gave the PLO a new regional and international stature, while forcing the Palestinian opposition onto the defensive.

In the view of the Islamic Jihad, the Oslo Accords were a device designed to extract the PLO from its financial mire and satisfy 'Arafat's lust for power. The signing of the agreement signaled the end of the PLO as a legitimate liberation movement and its conversion into a political party with narrow interests. While Israel gained recognition for its existence and for its conquest of the territories under the guise of redeployment, the Palestinians got a narrow regime bereft of any ability to achieve independence and sovereignty.[3] The destructive implications of the Oslo Accords went beyond the renunciation of the rights of the Palestinians. They linked the economic and defense networks of Palestinian self-government to those of Israel, thereby constituting a springboard for Zionist control of the region.[4]

The movement also dismissed the PLO's argument that the regional balance of power precluded retaining a maximalist stance of absolute justice and necessitated adjustment to the limitations of an operative reality. In Shiqaqi's opinion, this was a defeatist approach that nurtured the illusion that the international community could be depended upon to pressure Israel for more concessions. It was an illusion on two accounts: first, Israel was a part of the West and a basic component of the world system that the US hoped to establish; and second, it was the international community that had created Israel and dispossessed the Palestinians from their land. In this vein, the Islamic Jihad's charter denounced international forums, such as the UN, as mere devices of the West to destroy Islam and to fight against the oppressed. "they legitimize evil and cancel out justice," the charter asserted.[5]

While the balance of power did not favor the Arabs, Shiqaqi acknowledged, this was not an eternal state and could be altered by staunch resistance: Nelson Mandela remained in prison for 27 years and never changed his position, ultimately going on to lead South Africa. Had he concerned himself with considerations of the balance of power, he could not have attained his impressive victory. The same was true of the liberation of the East European states from the oppressive yoke of Communism. It took the Jews themselves a thousand years to fulfill the dream of returning to Jerusalem and establishing their state. Therefore, Shiqaqi urged, the rationale that should guide the Arabs and Muslims should be that of the familiar Nasserist motto: "What was taken by force will be restored by force." The Arabs have vast resources at their disposal for this task: manpower, history, geography and a living ideology. It is Islam that bestows the historical dimension on the struggle for Palestine, with patience constituting the key word in this struggle.[6]

The religious delegitimation of the Oslo Accords, and the demand for establishing an alternative leadership for the Palestinians, put the Islamic Jihad on the opposite side of the divide from the PA, although without any impetus toward a full-fledged confrontation. On the contrary, the movement displayed cautious pragmatism in its relations with the PA, which adopted the rationale of a sovereign state anxious to enforce its rule in society. Shiqaqi even declared that his movement would intensify its civil activity in the PA territories and would consider establishing a political party. He noted, however, that it would not serve as a substitute for the Islamic Jihad nor lead to a halt in the armed struggle.[7]

The tendency of the Islamic Jihad toward ideological dogma in its political conduct was more pronounced than was the case for Hamas. This was the result of Islamic Jihad's elitist orientation and its small size. In effect, the movement's self-image as a vanguard force, along with skimpy resources, narrowed its range of strategic options. Its primary thrust was military activity against Israel, the source of the movement's legitimation within the Palestinian public. One of its publications stated explicitly that blood and self-sacrifice were the "personal capital" of the movement in the struggle over Palestine. In political terms, these two elements constituted the movement's *raison d'être* as well.[8] While Islamic Jihad military activity went back to the early 1980s, it was intensified in the wake of the Oslo Accords, climbing another notch (as with Hamas) with the perpetration of suicide attacks sanctified religiously as martyrdom. These attacks were influenced in no small measure by the Hizballah experience of the mid-'1980s.[9]

From the movement's point of view, suicide attacks, especially against a heretical government, fulfilled Islam faithfully, for the religion guarantees the *shahid* (martyr) a place in paradise. These attacks also served as an effective cover-up for the inferiority of the jihad fighters vis-à-vis Israel. Shiqaqi, addressing this issue, noted that the campaign against the enemy was multidimensional, hence it called for unconventional means.

The mistake of the resistance movement led by the PLO was that it tried to turn itself into a conventional army. By contrast, the goal of the suicide attacks was to create a "balance of fear" (*tawazin al-ru'b*) in order to neutralize, to the extent possible, the material balance of power in Israel's favor.[10] Yet, despite the ideological rationale behind such attacks, the Islamic Jihad did not remove them from the political context. This correlation was largely determined by the movement's emphasis on the organic unity between religion and politics, as well as by the fact that the cornerstone of the Oslo Accords was the security dimension.[11]

The suicide attacks, such as the one at Beit Lid junction near Netanya, which took the lives of 20 IDF soldiers (January 1995), engendered repressive measures by the PA, which allowed itself a freer hand in dealing with a relatively marginal element such as the Islamic Jihad. Not surprisingly, members of the Islamic Jihad were the first to be imprisoned by the PA security forces in early 1994 and charged with "harming the security of the homeland and the agreements signed by the PA." The detainees included the movement's highest-ranking leaders in the Gaza Strip, such as Nafidh 'Azzam, 'Abdallah al-Shami and Hani 'Abid.[12]

Along with military acts, the Islamic Jihad took two further steps in the political sphere during the post-Oslo Accords period. It strove to create a broad resistance front to the accords within the Palestinian opposition and among Islamic elements in the Middle East; and at the same time it sought an accommodation with the PA, emphasizing the necessity of avoiding civil war (*fitna*), which had had a traumatic effect in early Islam.

The Palestinian Opposition: Internal Strife

While united in its rejection of the Oslo Accords, the Palestinian opposition was fragmented on other issues. However, a sense of urgency regarding the need to put together an effective front against the accords led to the formation, in January 1994, of the Palestinian Forces Alliance (*Tahalluf al-Quwat al-Filastiniyya*), which replaced the "Ten Palestinian Factions" established two years previously. The formation of the new forum was a difficult process, primarily because of a demand by Hamas for weighted representation in the central leadership body, by virtue of its senior status. Ultimately, with intensive mediation by Shiqaqi, an agreement was reached over equal representation of all the member groups. The establishment of the Alliance constituted an admission of the failure of the "Ten Palestinian Factions," yet it did not portend any significant improvement in the poor functioning of the Palestinian opposition. In effect, the new body remained the same forum in a different garb. Its main contribution was in the rhetorical—rather than operative—sphere.[13] Even this contribution was minimal, giving the ideological differences between the religious and the secular camps over the future character of society once the occupation came to an end, as well as because of attempts by Hamas to turn the Palestinian opposition into a vehicle to enhance its status vis-à-vis the PLO. In this context, Fatah maintained an ongoing dialogue with the Palestinian left, especially with the DFLP and the PFLP, in order to convince them of the need to preserve the PLO framework and its leadership role. It thereby sought to neutralize Hamas efforts to set up a political, not only an ideological, alternative.[14]

Angered by Hamas' haughty approach, spokesmen for the Palestinian left also attacked Hamas' independent policy in connection with the armed struggle and its relations with the PA—e.g., its approval of an armistice with Israel (*hudna*) subject to such conditions as the dismantling of the settlements and withdrawal from the territories. Responding, Hamas claimed that it strove for close coordination with the other forces in the Alliance but found itself largely alone, as the leftist factions were weak and not sufficiently determined to foil Fatah's hold in Palestinian civil society. Put even more sharply, Hamas leader Mahmud al-Zahhar of the Gaza Strip charged that the coordination among opposition elements had failed because their positions were changeable and subject to self-interest, in contrast to that of Hamas, which was firm and consistent.[15]

The ideological differences within the Palestinian Forces Alliance were clearly repressed, but they did not disappear. An explicit indication was the response by DFLP leader Na'if Hawatmeh to the American move in January 1995 to freeze the assets of the Palestinian "terror organizations" and seek the arrest of their leaders. In Hawatmeh's opinion, the White House failed to distinguish between Islamic terror organizations, which rejected peace with Israel, and moderate organizations such as the DFLP, which sought a realistic settlement between the two sides.[16]

In Shiqaqi's view, the impotence of the Palestinian Forces Alliance stemmed from the ideological incompatibility among the groupings that made it up—Islamic, pan-Arab and Marxist—some of them beset by internal problems that affected the conduct of their struggle. Moreover, he stated, in contrast to the PLO, the Palestinian opposition found itself without international or regional backing for the first time. What was required was an end to mutual suspicion and claims to exclusive legitimacy; radical reforms in each group to eliminate manifestations of despotic leadership and bureaucratic corruption; and the consolidation of a clearly defined alternative to the Oslo Accords.[17]

Clearly, most of Shiqaqi's criticism was aimed at the leftist factions, although he also hinted at reservations about Hamas' pretensions to the leadership of the Palestinian opposition. In his view, while the proportional weight of each group in the Alliance should not be ignored, the key element must be the platform of the struggle itself, rather than control by a single organization that had yet to prove itself in terms of loyalty to the whole of Palestine.[18] The Islamic Jihad thus sought to strike back at Hamas for its efforts to participate in elections in the territories and for declarations by its top leaders, such as Ahmad Yasin, Mahmud al-Zahhar and Musa Abu Marzuq, regarding the possibility of a truce with Israel. According to Shiqaqi, the attempt to legitimize an armistice by referring to the *Hudaybiyya* accord which the Prophet had concluded with his rivals in Mecca was a distortion of the historic truth. First, that agreement did not involve the Jews. Second, the Prophet did not concede his land or his principles, and during the truce period entrenched the position of the Muslims by impressive conquests, culminating in his decisive campaign against Mecca.[19]

Indeed, the ideological convergence between the Islamic Jihad and Hamas that had emerged on the eve of the Intifada did not cancel out their political rivalry. This was evident after the Oslo Accords, even with the defensive position that both movements were forced to adopt. Hamas continued to view itself as the authentic exponent of Islam and to attack the Islamic Jihad's narrow perspective in terms of its exclusive reliance on armed struggle. Hamas attributed its own strength to the restraint it showed until the ripening of the reformist stage that it promoted in society. Only then did it take up military activity, which was much more effective and impressive than that of the Islamic Jihad. Retorting, Gazan

Islamic Jihad leaders Shami and 'Azzam argued that Islam was broad enough to contain several political trends, and that their own movement had not assimilated into Hamas because the justifications for its existence were still valid.[20]

The Islamic Jihad's disenchantment with the functioning of the Palestinian opposition was paralleled by disappointment in the absence of strategic depth in the Arab-Muslim world to back Palestinian Islam in its struggle against the Oslo Accords. This Arab-Muslim reticence had several causes. First, the Islamic movements in the countries of the Middle East were engaged in a struggle for their own existence, as in Syria and Algeria, or were preoccupied with heightening their integration into national politics, as in Egypt and Jordan. Most of these movements were satisfied with efforts to fuel anti-Israeli sentiment in the Arab street and express solidarity with the Palestinian cause and its standard-bearers. Second, the Arab regimes gave priority to their own political interests, and some—such as Egypt, Syria and Jordan—actually limited activity by the Palestinian opposition in their domains. Jordan showed particular determination in this, a reflection of the violent confrontations with the PLO there in the late 1960s, still deeply etched in the country's national consciousness.[21]

The acquisition of a supportive base in the region was more problematic for the Islamic Jihad than for Hamas, in light of the Islamic Jihad's delegitimation of Arab regimes (save for those that granted it patronage, such as Syria and Libya). Equally problematic was the deterrent aspect of its affinity with Shi'i Iran. Shiqaqi aptly described this limitation when he observed that the road to Palestine is blocked for the Islamic Jihad fighters by a double siege: an Israeli siege imposed through military means, and an Arab one consisting of preventive detention in the neighboring Arab states, especially Egypt and Jordan.[22] The movement complained about its scarce resources from time to time, e.g., in an appeal to readers of its organ, al-Mujahid, to help it expand through donations. It emphasized, however, that scarcity of means did not weaken its ideological tenacity, as phrased in one of its publications: "Few numerically, strong ideologically."[23]

Fragile Coexistence with the PA: Issues of Civil Society and Democracy

The absence of sufficient outside support, coupled with the struggle for political survival at home vis-à-vis both the PA and Israel, prompted the Islamic Jihad to seek a modus vivendi with the PA so as to enable continued military activity without clashing with the Authority. According to Nafidh 'Azzam, the existence of both the Islamic Jihad and the PA on the same territory required dialogue and mutual understanding.[24] The PLO, for its part, sought the co-option of the Islamic camp. This was especially pronounced in the early months of the formation of the Authority, when the PLO wanted to entrench its status and acquire bargaining chips for the peace negotiations with Israel. The PLO was in a situation of some distress over the religious issue for two reasons: the withdrawal of Islamic figures from its ranks following the Oslo Accords, including PNC president 'Abd al-Hamid al-Sa'ih and Islamic Jihad-Jerusalem leader As'ad Bayyud al-Tamimi;[25] and the absence of an official religious body to legitimize its policy, such as existed in certain Arab states. A promising source of such support was the Supreme Muslim Council, but many of its shaykhs continued to disapprove of the peace talks with Israel.[26]

The Islamic Jihad, in its contacts with PA representatives, made it clear that it had no intention of taking part in PA bodies in view of its rejection of the Oslo Accords on religious grounds. Nevertheless, the movement emphasized, it was determined to preserve its involvement with the local population and their needs. While refusing to take part in the general elections planned for January 1996, the Islamic Jihad explicitly demanded participation in the municipal elections, with the intention of serving the citizenry regardless of internal or external politics. It stated that any attempt to drive a wedge between it and society would be viewed as warning signal, as would the confiscation of weapons or damage to its civic assets, such as mosques.[27]

The differentiation between political activity under the aegis of the PA, which it rejected, and legitimate civil activity, was aimed at allowing the Islamic Jihad greater involvement with the population in order to recruit support vis-à-vis the PA. In the contest for public support, the movement focused on the PA's poor performance in all that pertained to building up a qualitative society and attaining genuine sovereignty. Detailed reports of the PA's deficiencies in the administrative and social areas appeared repeatedly in the movement's publications. These failures included the dire condition of hospitals, water pollution in the refugee camps, and neglect of the problem of Palestinian prisoners in Israeli jails. Summarizing the first year of the PA's performance, 'Abdallah al-Shami pointed to retrogression rather than progress in most areas of Palestinian life. Politically, the PA's brand of democracy was limited and turned the notion of the rule of law into a hollow slogan. Economically, unemployment increased, while the police and security forces expanded significantly. There were manifestations of corruption and a decline in public morality, as evidenced by the opening of pubs and the sale of alcoholic beverages.[28]

The movement perceived a strong link between the achievement of political stability and economic development, on the one hand, and the entrenchment of democracy on the other. It pointed out that the peace process and international aid alone would not create a democratic society. What was needed was a definition of the relationship of government to civil society. This should be achieved, first and foremost, by means of drawing up a constitution that would guarantee basic freedoms and allow institutional pluralism in the form of political parties, trade unions, charitable councils, etc. Only then would a positive transition to democracy be possible.[29]

In principle, scholars have pointed out, the hallmark of civil society is the existence of voluntary autonomous institutions that serve as a buffer between the state and the citizen. This was not only an institutional concept but a cultural one as well. It went beyond a decentralized political system, which limited the state's role to ensuring public order, to include cultural pluralism, i.e., qualitative public debate that involved tolerance for a wide range of political views. Accepting the notion of civil society, therefore, meant accepting the premise that no individual or group had a monopoly on truth. Nurturing such a society also involved the entrenchment of democracy, whose supreme test lay in the existence of measures to protect minorities from the obduracy of the majority.[30]

Civil society in the modern Middle East has been weak in light of the tight control of most of the Arab governments and the centralized economic structures that they built, which together discouraged free civic activity in society. With the fall of Communism and the democratization of Eastern Europe in the late 1980s, the notion of civil society was given a certain impetus in the Arab world. Arab leaders, as in Egypt and Jordan, showed a readiness to institute political liberalism, albeit one that was equivocal and reversible. Their primary motivation was the need to neutralize social pressures for greater political participation, rather than an espousal of the pluralistic democratic ethos. Yet, the electoral success of the Islamic Salvation Front (FIS) in Algeria in 1991, which later led to bloodshed, and the rise to power of the Welfare Party in Turkey in 1996, acted as a brake on the further liberalization of Arab politics. Similarly, the enthusiasm of the standard-bearers of the democratic ethos in the intellectual community cooled in light of the rising Islamic challenge, for fear of exchanging one authoritarian regime for another, possibly worse.[31]

Nevertheless, the notion of civil society (*al-mujtama' al-madani*) has become a key concept in political discourse in the Middle East in recent years, including in the Palestinian arena, where it has been placed on the agenda of both the PA and the opposition. Clearly, the fact that the notion of civil society warranted such attention on the part of both the Islamic Jihad and Hamas stemmed from the policies adopted by the PA toward the Islamic opposition. It merits further attention here.

With the signing of the Oslo Accords, the focus of Palestinian politics shifted from the Arab diaspora to the territories. The PLO became an internal player, striving to replace Israeli occupation with national governance under its own leadership. This process enhanced the status of the PLO both in the Middle East and in the rest of the world, but entailed complex internal challenges, especially the enforcement of its authority and the development of state institutions.

The PA, founded in July 1994, evoked a change in the status of the PLO from a resistance movement to the ruling elite of an evolving state. The shift, however, was partial and problematic. It did not eliminate the flaws that plagued the organization beforehand, such as administrative dysfunction, corruption and centralized decision-making. On the contrary, the organization assimilated these flaws into the PA. Moreover, realities in the territories posed other stumbling blocks to the development of a modern society, namely a delicate social composition marked by interregional (Gaza Strip-West Bank) and intergroup (urban, rural and refugee camp) tensions, and the retention of traditional social norms such as patriarchy. The inherent weaknesses in the PLO, combined with a fragile reality in the territories, made for defective functioning by the PA. It failed to fulfill Palestinian expectations for a better future under a national government.[32]

One of the primary areas of conflict between the Authority and local society centered on the issue of democracy. Upon its formation, the PA made plain that a firm stance in negotiations with Israel and a show of strength toward dissident groups at home were indispensable in the formative stages of the national entity. All the rest, including promoting democracy and pluralism in society, were secondary. This conceptual correlation between the success of the peace process in fulfilling the dream of a sovereign state, and internal stability, produced a centralized system that did not differ much from the pattern of other Arab states. Signs of this approach included a heavy reliance on the security forces, the establishment of special state-security courts and a state monopoly of the electronic media.[33]

Spokesmen projected the PA as a governmental framework whose authority was beyond appeal. While any political group in the territories could join PA bodies, or function as a legal opposition, none had the right to challenge the Authority's legitimacy or seek to replace it. This determination to enforce its authority over society also dictated the PA stance regarding the Islamic opposition.

Ever since its formation, the PA viewed the Islamic opposition, especially Hamas, as a significant threat to its status in the territories. Hence it tried to limit the strength of the Islamists through co-option (e.g., by offering key positions and by conducting a "national dialogue") along with political and physical pressure. However, the offensive against the Islamic opposition never reached the level of violent confrontation, as 'Arafat needed to recruit maximal public support against Israel. Rather, it was meant primarily to redefine the legitimate activity of Hamas and the Islamic Jihad in light of the existence of a central authority. As a high-ranking figure in the PA put it: "We are for pluralism and human rights, but against a multiplicity of authorities."[34] Deviations from the rules dictated by the PA regarding Islamic activity generally met with detentions, instant trials and the closure of newspapers and associations, the last, however, on a temporary basis.

It was this repressive context that largely fueled the impetus of the Islamic opposition to promote the cause of civil society in Palestinian politics. Shiqaqi went to extremes in praising civil society in Muslim history, especially during its formative era, which, he pointed out, curbed repressive state power by placing legislation, education, *waqf* (religious endowment) and market supervision in the hands of the 'ulama'. This practice prevented the moral corruption of the subjects, while preserving their conformity to religious values. Nowadays, in light of Westernization as well as a repressive government, the need was to assure that the fields of culture and education were not controlled solely by the state, so that the nation's "ideological independence" would be preserved.[35] Shiqaqi thus emphasized the structural dimension of civil society, i.e., its firm stance against government while also functioning as a means for promoting ideological unity.[36]

In essence, Shiqaqi advocated giving the Islamic state a more interventionist character than that envisioned by civil society, which, as Ernest Gellner has argued, holds no monopoly on truth or supervision over social conduct. Shiqaqi's view was shared by the religious establishment as well as by Islamists who had joined the PA. It was based on the premise of intimate relations between religion and politics in Islam in which the state is a functional entity whose primary legitimacy lies in the enactment of religious ordinances.[37] Referring to this premise, Shiqaqi noted that any attempt to divest Islam of its political content would mean leaving Muslims without identity and power.[38] He argued that secularism originated in Europe as a protest against the repressive rule of the church over social and political life. Applying this concept to the Islamic context was possible only under two conditions: that the church and its leaders be identified with the mosque and the 'ulama' in function and historical record; and that the bourgois social force, which fomented the break with Christianity and created the industrial revolution, be identified with a similar force in Muslim history. Clearly, neither of these conditions existed in the Islamic context. Thus, the premise is alien and endangers the very existence of Islam as a total way of life.[39]

The emphasis on the implicit link between Islam and politics also informed Shiqaqi's attitude to the issue of democracy. In several essays on Islam and democracy, he attacked the attempt by Western officials and observers to demonize the Islamic trend and to identify it with terror and hostility toward anyone who was democratic. In his view, the Islamic trend did not deny the faith of those who were not part of it; the title "Islamic" merely indicated a focus on Islamic activity in politics. The trend rejected violence as a means of implementing the Shari'a and the establishment of an Islamic state. On the contrary, it was the state that resorted to violence and denied the Islamists the freedom of self-expression and assembly enjoyed by other political groups, despite its broad public support. The offensive against Islamists, Shiqaqi pointed out, had the backing of the West, which was not interested in true democracy in the region because democracy meant the return of the masses—and with it Islam— to political power. Western countries had distanced themselves from China in the wake of the massacre of students at Tiananmen Square in 1990, and had supported Boris Yeltsin in the 1991 revolution in Russia. Yet, the West sided with the military regime in Algeria against the will of the people when the Islamic victory there was nullified. Democracy, Shiqaqi concluded, was relative. It was granted to all the countries of the world except those in the Middle East.[40]

Essentially, Shiqaqi held, the Islamic trend sanctified freedom and political participation based on the *shura*,[41] but rejected the Western meaning of democracy as popular sovereignty and the separation between religion and politics. Man is charged with building this world, but he does so only within the context of recognition of the superiority of divine law. Quoting Hasan al-Banna, founder of the Muslim Brothers in Egypt, Shiqaqi noted that government in Islam is civil governance based on the ruler's responsibility to the community, while also integrating experts in public and worldly affairs. Banna did not object to political pluralism, but he was highly critical of the conduct of parties in Egypt in his time (the 1930s and '40s), for they lacked any ideological platform or affinity to the people. He also supported the notion of freedom of opinion, although this was limited to those aspects of Islam that were open to human reason and endeavor, i.e., instances where the sacred text was unclear.

Addressing the sensitive issue of the status of minorities under the Islamic government, Shiqaqi limited himself to a statement that the *dhimmi*s (protected subjects) benefited from tolerance and welfare in Muslim society. He cited Muslim theologian Ibn Hazzam (d. 1064) who related that the Kharijites had forced heresy on Muslims and killed many of them, yet insisted on paying for a date palm they had taken from a Christian even though he had offered it to them for free. Shiqaqi observed: "If this was the way of an Islamic group that was one of the most extreme in Muslim history, one can rest assured about the position of the broad Islamic trend, which shuns violence, regarding the minorities."[42]

Summarizing the relationship between Islam and democracy, Shiqaqi emphasized that the Islamic trend was the first victim of the absence of democracy in the region. It sought to achieve statehood by democratic means, in contrast to the existing regimes, which made their way by the use of force. When the Islamic trend is in government, Shiqaqi pledged, it will "preserve the democratic character of the state, while honoring the will of the nation and the law."[43] Several conclusions may be drawn from Shiqaqi's arguments:

1. The essence of his thinking related to clearing the Islamic movements of accusations that they were a threat to democracy, rather than to an elaborate discussion of the nature of government they would install if they attained power, or the extent of liberty they would allow dissident parties. He confined himself to an assertion that the legitimacy of every opinion or grouping in society derived from its respect for the statutory position of the Qur'an as the law of the land. This was expressed even more pointedly by Bashir Nafi' and Muhammad al-Hindi, who held that any political grouping not based on Islam was illegitimate and must be opposed.[44]

2. Shiqaqi advocated change and openness, but also restricted them when they challenged religious conviction or moral conduct. He promoted human endeavor, yet subjected it to theological sanctions by virtue of the organic unity between religion and politics in Islam. He approved of the liberation of man from the bonds of materialism and enslavement to his fellow men, but supported the subjugation of man's will to the "sanctification of the absolute" and the needs of the collective.[45]

3. The guarantee of minority rights under an Islamic government, as outlined by Shiqaqi, did not entirely clarify whether this included full integration in the majority Muslim society, including exemption from the *jizya* (poll tax) or holding high-ranking public posts. Hamas spokesmen, by comparison, provided an explicit negative (albeit apologetic) answer. According to Jamil Hamami, a West Bank Hamas leader, the terms *dhimmis* and *jizya* should not be nullified, although some contemporary 'ulama' believed that they should be relegated to history. The term *dhimmi* expresses respect for the religion of the other, while the term *jizya* refers to financial compensation by non-Muslims for public services and ex-

empts them from the defense of the homeland. They can remove this tax by requesting a part in the task of defense, as occurred historically during the Islamic conquests.[46]

Indeed, the advocacy of democracy and civil society also entailed a pragmatic dimension, reflecting the distress of the Islamic Jihad and its awareness of the superior power of the PA. Hamas, too, acknowledged that the embrace of democracy was necessary to win over public opinion, and downplayed its negative aspects. This was aptly expressed by Hamas leader Shaykh Jamal Salah, who pointed out that the *shura* was in force only where an Islamic government existed. In its absence, the faithful had two alternatives: democracy or dictatorship.[47] By contrast, the third largest Islamic group in the territories, the Liberation Party, rejected democracy out of hand, branding it a "heretical regime." Its argument was that democracy was identified with the West and must therefore be viewed as a form of cultural invasion. Moreover, democracy was the product of man, who, in contrast to Allah, was fallible.[48] Notably, the Liberation Party, a negligible element in Palestinian politics, could allow itself to cling to dogma, in contrast to the Islamic Jihad, and all the more so Hamas.

Seeking to overcome its inferior position vis-à-vis the PA, the Islamic Jihad, like Hamas, worked out a modus vivendi in its relations with 'Arafat, which it justified by the religious injunction against civil war. Spokesmen for the Islamic Jihad pointed out that the controversy with the PA was ideological and political, warranting a solution through dialogue and not violence, which was to be reserved for Israel alone.[49] The movement's leaders in the territories, such as 'Abdallah al-Shami, Nafidh 'Azzam, Muhammad al-Hindi, Yusuf al-'Arif and 'Abd al-Halim 'Izz al-Din, displayed a pronounced desire for accommodation with the PA. These figures had felt the heavy hand of the PA more than once, especially following criticism of it or attacks carried out against Israel, and were closer to the main arena of events than the leadership in exile.

Shami, who was arrested on suspicion of inciting one of the suicide bombers in the Beit Lid incident (January 1995) but was released shortly thereafter, declared that the PA had become part of the Palestinian reality. He added that his movement was considering temporarily shelving its military attacks against Israel launched from the self-rule zones. Shiqaqi, in response, insisted that military activity would continue, and that dozens of candidates for suicide attacks were waiting in line. He requested clarification from Shami regarding his remarks, which he defined as a "private opinion" not binding on the movement. In the wake of this reprimand, Shami published a statement that there was no split or controversy in the ranks of the movement and no change in its policy toward the armed struggle in Palestine. This was promptly followed by a statement by Nafidh 'Azzam confirming that any decision on freezing the military attacks or reaching an agreement with the PA was the sole prerogative of the Islamic Jihad leadership outside the territories.[50]

This episode pointed to the inherent tension between the "outside" and "inside" leaders of the Islamic Jihad over the issue of armed struggle and the attitude toward the PA. The tension, however, remained largely latent, due to Shiqaqi's dominant leadership. Similar but more visible tension existed between the "outside" and "inside" leaders of Hamas, especially because of its populist and heterogeneous character and the fact that its most senior leader, Ahmad Yasin, was imprisoned in Israel. Not surprisingly, most of the rifts occurred within Hamas rather than in the Islamic Jihad. This was manifested in the withdrawal of key figures from Hamas and the formation of new factions, mostly ephemeral, that operated in the PA orbit. Such fissures were also a reflection of the partial success of 'Arafat's policy of co-option, especially among Hamas 'ulama' in the West Bank. Examples were Shaykhs Hamid al-Bitawi, Jamal Mansur, Jamal Salim and Tallal Sidr, all of whom had been on good terms with nationalist elements and were formally identified with the Jordanian religious establishment. They did not view their shift to the PA as a deviation from their basic conception of the struggle over Palestine, which ranged from jihad to *da'wa*, depending on the constraints of reality. In their thinking, joining the PA was legitimate because it was based on applying the principle of *ijtihad* in political matters, which, as distinct from matters of worship, is flexible and aims at improving the welfare of the people (*maslaha*).[51]

In the case of the Islamic Jihad, the tactical shift in balance between jihad and *da'wa* was more limited because of the movement's focus on military rather than communal activity. The result was a tendency toward greater dogmatism in the movement's policy and less success by the PA in co-opting its followers. The Jihad factions that did operate in the PA context, such as the al-Aqsa Brigades headed by Fa'iz al-Aswad, and the

Islamic Jihad in Palestine headed by Muhammad Abu Samara, remained satellite groups with no political weight.[52] Their pronounced loyalty to the PA and its peace policy[53] was largely attributable to their membership composition—former activists in Fatah or in leftist groups, who had internalized Islam as complementary to Palestinian nationalism. The subordination of Islam to national goals meant the shift of supremacy to state-sponsored Islam—which served the interests of the political elite—over dissident Islam.

The Islamic Jihad's modus vivendi with the PA underwent a severe jolt in the wake of military attacks carried out by members of the movement, e.g., following Israel's alleged murder of Hani 'Abd (November 1994). The Islamic Jihad was also the target of arrests and repression in the wake of the heightened conflict between the PA and Hamas.[54] Responding to severe measures taken against it, the Islamic Jihad warned of the possibility that the Palestinian police, rather than fulfilling its normative role of preserving public order and ensuring civil liberties, was being used by the PA as a means to entrench a dictatorship. The movement pointed out that the Palestinian people, who did not recognize an oppressive regime, would not restrain themselves for long.[55] This emphasis on the distinctiveness of the Palestinian people as loyal to freedom, pluralism and democracy, revealed signs of a movement on the defensive.

The PA's repression of the Islamic opposition was essentially part of a test of 'Arafat's leadership, and reflected his desire to prove to both the US and Israel that he was indeed fighting terror, as required by the Oslo Accords. Yet it also reflected the rationale of a sovereign state. This was clearly expressed by the head of the Palestinian police in the Gaza Strip, Nasir Yusuf, who noted, "The opposition insists on its right to oppose the occupation, and we insist on our duty to maintain the agreements that we have signed." Elaborating on this theme, the Fatah secretary-general in the Gaza Strip, Diyab al-Luh, observed that "Fatah filled the role of national liberation, and today fills the role of building of the homeland."[56]

The rationale of a sovereign state was further reinforced in the wake of the general elections for the presidency of the PA and for the Palestinian Legislative Council held in January 1996,[57] which were boycotted by the Palestinian opposition. The Islamic Jihad, like Hamas, tried to minimize the importance of the elections and their results, labeling them "formalistic democracy" designed to legitimize the Oslo Accords. Moreover, the Islamic Jihad stated that it would carry on the armed struggle and would also take part in elections for civil bodies that served the community.[58] Its followers drew encouragement from the disappointment of wide sectors of the Palestinian public with the deficient performance of the PA and the lack of significant improvement in socioeconomic matters. Another source of encouragement was the joint Islamic Jihad-Hamas success in trade union and academic campus elections. The student sector, tending traditionally toward political activism, served as a focus of protest against PA domestic policy and against Israel.[59]

While the Islamic Jihad was overshadowed by the broader-based Hamas, this fact also served as a source of strength for it: Hamas successes in its political rivalry with the PA and in its attacks on Israel, indirectly legitimized the status of Islamic Jihad within the Palestinian Islamist camp. On more than one occasion, the movement enfolded Hamas fatalities as its own, thereby basking in the wide public support for Hamas.[60]

On the whole, the Islamic Jihad remained loyal to its overall strategy regarding the struggle for Palestine. However, the existence of a political entity in the throes of state-building posed new limitations, particularly with the murder of the movement's leader, Fathi al-Shiqaqi, in Malta by Israeli Mossad agents in October 1995.

The Movement after Shiqaqi's Death

Shiqaqi was the most prominent figure in the small and highly centralized Islamic Jihad movement. It was he who outlined movement policy, supervised operational and financial affairs, and maintained most of the contacts with various elements in the Palestinian and regional arena. The Islamic Jihad developed an institutional structure made up of a general congress, an advisory council and a general secretariat, to which the movement often referred as reflecting its democratic essence. However, the extent of the practical functioning of this structure was unclear. Shiqaqi's charismatic leadership engendered strong ideological and political cohesion within the movement, leaving a limited field of maneuver for the internal leadership in its contacts with the PA. Other founding fathers of the movement, including 'Abd al-Aziz 'Awda, Taysir al-Khatib and Sayyid Baraka, found themselves shunted aside and accused Shiqaqi of imitating 'Arafat's style of one-man leadership, using security reasons as an excuse.[61]

Voicing indirect yet clear criticism, 'Awda pointed out that one factor behind Islam's victories over its enemies in its early period was the equality achieved between the Prophet and his fighters. Each fighter felt that the Prophet, by virtue of his closeness to them, had the same duties and the same rights as they. The Prophet involved them in his decisions, thereby instilling in them a sense of shared responsibility.[62] A more profound and blunt attack against Shiqaqi's centralist conduct came from Baraka, who officially withdrew from the movement in 1991.[63]

Shiqaqi, in a laconic response, attributed the numerous reports of rifts within the movement to an intensive campaign of delegitimation conducted against it by the US, Israel and the PA in order to erode its internal unity. Differences of opinion and occasional problems exist in every party, he stated, especially in light of the difficulties involved in operating in complex regional circumstances. However, in the case of the Islamic Jihad, these did not detract from ideological and political cohesion, he claimed.[64]

The movement's strong identification with Shiqaqi had a negative effect on its functioning after his death. In Max Weber's idiom, the Islamic Jihad had not experienced a "routinization of charisma" under Shiqaqi, i.e., a process in which the relative strength of personal charismatic leadership gives way to regular functioning within permanent institutions.[65] The hasty appointment of Shiqaqi's successor, Ramadan Shalah, as secretary-general, alongside the mythologization of Shiqaqi's image that developed, were intended in part to cover up the shock to the movement caused by his death.[66] Shiqaqi himself was quoted as saying: "I am not worried about the Islamic Jihad after my death. We have built a strong infrastructure." In practical terms, this meant the continuation of the armed struggle against Israel, as exemplified by two suicide attacks carried out by the movement against IDF forces in the Gaza Strip (2 November 1995).[67]

Shiqaqi's funeral, which took place in Damascus in the presence of over 40,000 persons, quickly turned into a rally against Israel and the US. It brought together the leaders of the Palestinian opposition and high-ranking personalities from Iran and the Hizballah, who came to pay respects to Shiqaqi. Symbolic funeral services were also held in the territories, with senior representatives of the PA calling at the mourners reception area set up in the Gaza Strip. Shiqaqi's successor, Shalah, pledged to continue in his footsteps, declaring at the grave that "the armed struggle will remain the only path of the Islamic Jihad."[68]

Ramadan Shalah, born in the Shaja'iyya quarter of Gaza City, an important stronghold of the movement, was a member of the Islamic Jihad founding group back in the early 1970s, during their student days in Egyptian universities. Since then, most of his activity in the movement had taken place outside the territories, and had been integrated with his academic specialization in political science, first in London and later in Florida, where he earned a doctorate. With the outbreak of the Intifada in 1987, Shalah returned to London and, together with Bashir Nafi', directed the transfer of funding to the movement's branches in the territories while helping to draw up the movement's leaflets. He returned to the US in 1990, where he became head of the Institute for Research of Islam and the Middle East based in Tampa, Florida. He was also a founder of the Islamic Palestine Committee, which organized conferences and published materials in support of Islamic activity in Palestine. In 1994 he moved to Beirut, where he resided until his appointment in October 1995 as secretary-general of the movement upon Shiqaqi's murder.[69]

Assuming his new role, Shalah began to consolidate his leadership in order to neutralize the dissatisfaction in the movement ranks with his relative anonymity and the fact that he had spent most of his time in the West, far from the arena of the main events. This was also a source of criticism by most of the former leaders of the movement, such as Sayyid Baraka, who accused Shalah of being unable to assume a moral, collegial leadership style. Disappointed, Baraka stated that he felt a greater affinity to Hamas than to the Islamic Jihad.[70] While Hamas, as a mass movement, could allow itself internal disputes and even rifts without much harm to its firm status, the Islamic Jihad, with its scant resources and rivalry with other Jihad factions, had to display unity.

Shalah took several steps to dispel discontent internally and meet the external challenges. First, he emphasized his close acquaintance with Shiqaqi during their student days in Egypt in 1977, a relationship that he portrayed as a "rebirth" for himself. While asserting that he had been elected to the post by the movement's democratic bodies, Shalah noted that Shiqaqi had treated him as his natural successor.[71] A second step was to minimize the importance of the withdrawal of certain figures from the movement during Shiqaqi's era, which, Shalah claimed, had resulted from personal rather than ideological motives.[72] Third, he took a firm stand on the issue of the armed struggle and the peace process. He accused the PLO of moral bankruptcy and branded the PA "an ally of the occupation." In his opinion, the Palestinians were still in a stage of national liberation and required someone who could lead them in the struggle against the occupation rather than repress them.[73]

An awareness that continued attacks against Israel were the key to the existence of the movement, and thereby to the consolidation of Shalah's leadership, was reflected in a suicide attack in Tel Aviv on March 1996, close in time to two lethal attacks perpetrated by Hamas in Jerusalem and Ashkelon. The attack in Tel Aviv resulted in the death of 12 civilians and the wounding of some 100. However, energetic measures taken against the movement's infrastructure by the PA in response sapped its operational capabilities.[74] Moreover, Israeli measures, especially the imposition of a long military closure of the territories, evoked strong dissatisfaction by Palestinians who were reliant on the Israeli labor market for their livelihood. Shalah denied that the movement was in retreat, although he admitted that it was more exposed than ever to repressive measures both by Israel and the PA.[75]

The ascent of the right to power in Israel's elections in May 1996 resulted in an easing of pressure on the Islamic Jihad by the PA. However, expectations by the movement for renewed momentum on the part of the Palestinian opposition were disappointed. Internal strife continued, as reflected in the withdrawal by the PFLP and the DFLP from the Palestinian Alliance Forces in September 1996. The Islamic Jihad blamed the leftist factions for adopting a passive stance toward the Oslo Accords and the PA. It also accused Hamas of seeking compromise with the PA in order to ensure its civil institutions and denounced its leaders' ongoing declarations regarding the possibility of a truce with Israel.[76] According to *al-Istiqlal*, sanctifying an organizational framework obscured the duty of loyalty to Allah, while delaying the jihad in Palestine distorted Islam, which did not differentiate between jihad and other basic duties, e.g., prayer or fasting.[77]

Beyond sharpening the revolutionary message, these remarks were also intended to reemphasize the separate existence of the Islamic Jihad after its ideological distinctiveness had been blurred with the entry of Hamas into the circle of violence against Israel. This separate existence was acknowledged by Hamas leaders. Shaykh Ahmad Yasin, visiting Damascus shortly after his release from prison in Israel (October 1997), went to Shiqaqi's grave and praised him as a "symbol for the Muslim believer and a true fighter." The dispute with him, Yasin asserted, was over methods of activity, not over principles. Other Hamas personalities emphasized that the Palestinian arena was broad enough to accommodate several Islamic movements. With such statements, Hamas sought to demonstrate its tolerance of the Islamic Jihad, but also to highlight the obvious asymmetry in the relative strength of the two in society.[78]

Chapter Five:
Relations with Iran and Hizballah

The initial admiration of Sunni radicals for the Islamic Revolution in Iran—for its emphasis on political activism and its ecumenical message—proved naive and hasty. Within a year of the revolution, this admiration had faded away almost entirely, to be replaced by a sense of enmity. The main reasons were the discord within the Iranian religious elite; Iranian indifference toward the 'Alawite Syrian regime's massacre of the Muslim Brothers in Hamah (1982); and the outbreak of the Iran-Iraq War, which quickly assumed the image of a Persian-Arab and Shi'i-Sunni conflict.

Sunni radicals viewed these developments as concrete evidence of revolutionary Iran's inability to actualize an ideal Islamic society. These developments further seemed to attest to Khomeini's ongoing adherence to Shi'i traditions, which perpetuated separation from the Sunna and reduced the pan-Islamic vision to belligerent rhetoric.[1] Shi'i distinctiveness—which Shi'is saw as underlying the success of the revolution, but Sunnis viewed as the cause of its deviance[2]—limited Iranian influence to the narrow sphere of the Shi'i communities in the Middle East. While Islamic movements in the Arab world continued to treat the Islamic Revolution as a source of inspiration in the struggle against domestic oppression and foreign imperialism, they rejected the messages of the revolution and delegitimized Khomeinism.[3] According to Sa'id Hawwa, a leader of the Muslim Brothers in Syria, the Islamic Revolution was not a victory for Islam, but a retreat, because of its adoption of deviant and anti-Sunni Shi'i concepts. These included the denunciation of the Sahaba (the companions of the Prophet), refuting the Hadith (the Prophet's sayings) as an obligatory judicial foundation, and the eschatology of the return of the hidden and infallible Imam. Khomeini, by incorporating these concepts, took up the thread of the apostate movements in Muslim history (*zandaqah*), thereby weakening the Islamic nation, Hawwa charged. Far from constituting a beacon of truth, strength and freedom, Khomeini's Iran became a country of falsehood, degeneration and slavery.[4]

In light of radical Sunni animosity toward Iran, which exposed the residual historic hostility between Sunna and Shi'a, the Islamic Jihad stood out as a group steeped in the Sunni tradition yet displaying pronounced pro-Iranian leanings. Until the outbreak of the Intifada, the Islamic Jihad's affinity for Iran was anchored in two spheres: (1) Ideological—loyalty to Khomeini's pan-Islamic approach, which strove for both the unity of the Muslim world and the liberation of Palestine. This loyalty prompted minimizing the sectarian differences between Sunna and Shi'a while internalizing the revolution's terminology (such as jihad and martyrdom). (2) Political—loyalty to Khomeini's charismatic leadership and a willingness to hand over the reins of the Muslim world to him.

The events of the Intifada in late 1987, and the shift of the Islamic Jihad leadership to Lebanon and Syria, led to a material dependence on Iran as well. This was reflected in financial and logistic aid disbursed through the Iranian Embassy in Beirut and through Hizballah, and in effect placed the Islamic Jihad under the patronage of Iran. The movement's exiled leaders, Shiqaqi and 'Awda, appearing in the media spotlight and in encounters with Iranian diplomats in Beirut and Damascus, expressed unreserved support for the Iranian revolution.[5] Shiqaqi praised Iran's contribution and that of the Islamic resistance in Lebanon to the advancement of the struggle in Palestine and the restoration of the glory of the Muslim nation.

> The philosophy of sacrifice that is applied daily is what has protected Islam and advanced it day after day toward the liberation of man and the downfall of the haughty. It is the philosophy of sacrifice that has created our glory and our pride. In contrast, the philosophy of the preachers of half the way is what causes our defeat.... We shall continue the Intifada until we liberate our land from the sea to the river and establish our Islamic state as part of our Muslim homeland. I pray to Allah to protect Imam Khomeini so that he will enter Palestine and we shall hand over the keys of Nazareth and Jerusalem to him and pray together in the al-Aqsa mosque.[6]

The existence of a pro-Iranian group that evoked sympathy among the Palestinians, along with the Islamic imprint of the Intifada, provided a renewed impetus to Iran's efforts to extricate itself from its isolation in the Arab Sunni world. Granting wide media coverage to the Intifada, Iran accentuated its role in the development of the Palestinian Islamic Jihad and claimed proprietorship over the Intifada. According to the pro-Iranian organ *al-Thawra al-Islamiyya* (London), "The only available path for the Palestinian people is sacrifice for Allah. History shows that the strength of peoples is not in their weaponry but in their faith."[7]

In Iran's view, the Intifada, along with the parallel struggles in Iran and Lebanon, exposed not only the perseverance of the "reactionary" Arab regimes in curtailing Islamization in the region, but also the impotence of the PLO leadership. Iran thereby voiced its aversion for the PLO, which had adopted an ambivalent stance regarding the Islamic Revolution and had disappointed Iranian expectations.[8] The official Iranian press agency, commenting on the PLO, announced: "Groups that stand for conciliation and opportunism must not be allowed to lead the Intifada. They must be attuned to the general desire to adopt Islam; otherwise their leaders will be removed from the ranks of the people."[9]

The Iranian attack on the PLO was accompanied by concerted but unsuccessful attempts to establish an alternative pro-Iranian Palestinian leadership that would undermine Fatah and destroy its hold in Lebanon and the territories. This alternative leadership was to include exiled representatives of the Islamic Jihad as well as leaders of the Palestinian rejection front such as Ahmad Jibril, Sa'id Musa Muragha (Abu Musa) and Sabri al-Banna (Abu Nidal). Central figures reported to be involved in these efforts were Iranian Foreign Minister 'Ali Akbar Velayati; the head of the Information Agency, Ahmad Jannati; and the former leader of the Lebanese Islamic Jihad, 'Imad Mughniyya. In response, the mufti of Jerusalem, Shaykh Sa'd al-Din al-'Alami, and Palestinian ambassador in Iraq 'Azzam al-Ahmad denounced attempts to foment friction between the Palestinians and emphasized that the PLO was composed of all the Palestinian political streams.[10]

Seeking to expand its support of the struggle for Palestine and thus gain a foothold in the Sunni world, Iran also organized conferences of solidarity with the Intifada. High-ranking religious figures and other delegates of Islamic movements from the Arab-Muslim world participated. The most important of these took place in Tehran (14–22 October 1991) under the sponsorship of the Iranian parliament, with the conspicuous presence of the entire Iranian leadership. The Tehran event, timed to precede the convening of the Madrid peace conference, was attended by delegations from some 40 Muslim countries, including leaders of Islamic Jihad, Hizballah, al-Nahda in Tunis, the Brothers movements in Jordan and Egypt, and Hamas.[11] The presence of a representative of Hamas at the conference was a significant milestone in furthering dialogue between Hamas and Iran.[12]

During the course of the conference, a *fatwa* was issued, pronouncing the relinquishing of jihad for the liberation of Palestine and Jerusalem to be forbidden and criminal. The final communique termed Israel an illegal entity, whose presence in the heart of Muslim land constituted an evil design by world Zionism against Islam. It called for unity among all the Palestinian fighting forces in uprooting the occupation, and ratified an annual allocation for the Intifada.[13]

Along with broad support for the Intifada, Iran fostered political ties with the exiled Islamic Jihad leaders. Iran's support enabled the movement to develop an infrastructure, mainly in Lebanon but also in other allied Arab countries, such as Syria and Sudan, which functioned as branches outside the territories for advancing the armed struggle against Israel. Iranian aid included the allocation of training camps, military guidance and funding movement publications. A key role was assigned to the Hizballah in Lebanon, which shared Khomeini's pan-Islamic vision and placed itself at the forefront of the struggle of Muslims against their oppressors. Like its patron, Hizballah declared its commitment to the liberation of all of Palestine and its support of the Intifada.[14] According to the movement's spiritual leader, Sayyid Muhammad Husayn Fadlallah, "the Palestinian problem epitomizes our entire history and our future. It is linked with all the blows suffered by the Muslims from world tyranny."[15] Reinforcing the Islamic Jihad's ecumenical stance, Fadlallah emphasized the need for convergence between Sunna and Shi'a and criticized the friction within the Palestinian opposition. The opposition factions, he charged, were interested only in their own survival.[16]

Despite the Islamic Jihad's commitment to overt political subversion, its proximity to Hizballah turned the movement into a quasi-military organization. This was reflected both in Shiqaqi's new title as secretary-general of the movement and the establishment of a military hierarchy, represented by a military spokesman.[17] Alongside material dependence on Hizballah, the Islamic Jihad developed an operational partnership with it, reflected in several joint attacks against Israel.[18] Unanimity regarding the centrality of Palestine and partnership in the armed struggle against Israel fostered a close-knit relationship between the two movements. This was well reflected in an obituary written by Shiqaqi in *al-Mujahid* upon the death of the Hizballah leader, 'Abbas al-Musawi, in February 1992:

> From the day of our first encounter I envied you and saw you as more of a Palestinian than I, bearing the concern for Palestine and the Intifada....Your blood consolidates us so that we will arise, cry out, fire our bullets at the breast of the enemy, and from your spilled blood extract a curse for the conqueror.[19]

The Islamic Jihad published a leaflet calling for a general strike in the territories and the Palestinian refugee camps in Lebanon as a sign of solidarity marking Musawi's death. It also took responsibility for a revenge attack in Jerusalem.[20] Two months later, the movement carried out an attack on IDF soldiers in South Lebanon (April 1992), followed by the publication of a joint manifesto with Hizballah, which declared: "We made an alliance with Allah, the Imam Khomeini, the leader of the Islamic nation al-Sayyid Khamene'i...to continue the jihad, despite the great sacrifices which may be required."[21]

The Islamic Jihad thus viewed itself as a promoter of Iran's pan-Islamic and anti-imperialistic vision, with Iran providing both an ideological inspiration and political backing. Iranian and Hizballah leaders also sanctioned the movement's suicide attacks, depicting them as legitimate measures against an illegitimate entity, while ignoring the other Palestinian Jihad factions.[22] From the Islamic Jihad's point of view, preserving close ties with Iran and Hizballah was designed to highlight the revolutionary potential of Islam in light of the weakness of the Islamic movements in the Arab Middle East.[23] Still, Islamic Jihad spokesmen tended to minimize the extent of Iranian patronage, aware that too close an identification with Tehran would damage the movement's attractiveness to the Sunni Palestinians and serve as a weapon for its political rivals, i.e., the PLO/PA. While Shiqaqi acknowledged that a resistance movement could not conduct a long campaign without sufficient resources, he denied that the major portion of the aid for his movement came from Iran. Iran's assistance, he said, was more political and moral than military, including financial support for the families of those killed in the Intifada.

Other leaders of the movement, such as Shami and 'Azzam in the Gaza Strip, emphasized that relations with Iran did not affect the movement's independent decision-making or its ties with other forces in the Middle East. In their view, Iran was a regional power that could not be ignored, and relations with it were based more on mutual respect than on one-sided domination.[24]

Indeed, the granting of patronage did not necessarily mean the receipt of total or unequivocal loyalty. Shiqaqi's charismatic leadership, combined with Iran's isolation in the regional arena, endowed the Islamic Jihad with maneuverability in its relations with its political patron. The movement emphasized that its relations with political powers in the Middle East were gauged by the extent of their attachment to Islam and Palestine. In the case of Iran, this attachment was authentic and consistent: Iran viewed Islam as a political system; it emphasized the centrality of Palestine and the duty to liberate it through armed jihad; and it called for pan-Islamic unity divested of any national dimension or factional identity.[25] Ideologically, the emphasis placed on the pan-Islamic image of Iran did not mean the introversion of the Shi'a but the reduction of differences between Shi'a and Sunna; politically, it meant the positioning of the Islamic Jihad at the center of the Islamic consensus in both the Palestinian and regional arenas.

In fact, the Islamic Jihad remained the only Palestinian movement which, since its inception in 1980, consistently pledged loyalty to the Iranian revolution.[26] Such loyalty placed the Islamic Jihad in a unique position among Sunni movements in the Arab world, forcing it to adopt an ongoing stance of self-justification. This dilemma was illustrated in the movement's appeal to Iran to show restraint in its mounting friction with the Taliban movement in Afghanistan, so as not to provide its enemies with a pretext to brand the Shi'a as instigators of war against the Sunna.[27]

Iran did not consistently maintain its commitment to pan-Islamic unity, and foiled its own efforts to improve relations with Sunni radicals during most of the 1980s. Khomeini never completely divested himself of Shi'i antagonism toward the Sunna. An additional source of friction was his depiction of himself as a replacement for the Hidden Imam, who, upon returning to the world, will complete the work of the Prophet Muhammad—a depiction perceived in Sunni circles as denigrating the exalted status of Muhammad as the last of the prophets. Moreover,

Khomeini and his successors displayed political pragmatism that did not necessarily conform to the revolutionary vision. This was best reflected in foreign policy, in light of the debilitating war with Iraq (1980–88), the deteriorating economy and the international siege engineered by the US.[28] Still, the vision of exporting the revolution was not abandoned. On the contrary, the rise of the Islamic movements as the primary challenge to Arab regimes in the 1980s alongside the momentum of the Middle East peace process, led Iran to re-emphasize the ecumenical message formulated by Khomeini. This was reflected in more concrete efforts to gain ground beyond the Shi'i communities of the Middle East, hitherto the main target for spreading the revolution. In practical terms, Iran increased support for radical Sunni activity in Algeria, Tunisia, Jordan and Palestine.[29]

Support for the Islamic movements, if only on the moral and political levels, constituted a major obstacle to the restoration of Iran's relations with the Arab states and, as a result, to its full integration into the regional system. Although Tehran, especially since the election of Muhammad Khatami as president (May 1997), sought to defuse the mutual animosity with the Arab world, its conciliatory approach did not herald an abandonment of its dissident allies in the Middle East, such as Sudan, Hizballah and Palestinian Islam. The supreme leader of Iran, Ayatollah 'Ali Khamene'i, was prepared to show flexibility in the economic area and in some aspects of foreign policy, especially in terms of relations with Europe, which displayed readiness to abandon its "critical dialogue." However, he was not inclined to end the hostility toward the US or the conflict with Israel in two major arenas—Lebanon and Palestine.[30]

In retrospect, the political capital gained by Tehran from its patronage of the Islamic Jihad was slight (as compared, for example, to its gains from Hizballah), especially in light of the movement's minimal influence in the territories and the rifts within its ranks following Shiqaqi's murder in 1995. Iran's leaders claimed Shiqaqi as their own martyr, declared a public day of mourning, and named a street after him. Their protégé, Hizballah leader Hasan Nasrallah, stated that "We are all soldiers of the Islamic Jihad."[31] None of this, however, blunted the Iranians' awareness that the movement had not lived up to their expectations.

Ostensibly, Hamas was a better and a more promising channel of influence in light of its grass roots in Palestinian society, but it, too, proved to be limited. Upon its emergence just before the Intifada, Hamas displayed indifference toward the Islamic Revolution, giving its loyalty to its own parent movement, the Brothers. The Hamas charter of 1988 contained no echo of Khomeini's philosophy or mention of Iran. Ideologically, this was reflected in an observation by Shaykh Khalil al-Quqa, a Hamas leader exiled in April 1988: "The Khomeinist stream is shallow and has ended. It has passed over Palestine as a light breeze, and as such left no impression worthy of mention."[32] Politically, Hamas' attitude to the Islamic Revolution was revealed in disdain toward supporters of Khomeini—the Islamic Jihad activists.

However, at the end of the 1980s, the ideological rigidity of Hamas made way for political pragmatism, in light of the waning of the Intifada and the accelerated peace process. This problematic context prompted Hamas to view Iran, which placed itself at the head of the camp opposed to the peace process, as an ally. Hamas' shift in position, based on pragmatic considerations, was articulated by Khalil al-Quqa, who in 1988 had been quoted as denying any Iranian influence in Palestine. In 1991, however, he declared that "the Islamic Revolution, in raising the banner of Islam, left an impact on the entire region and not only on the Islamic movement in Palestine."[33]

The primary force behind the strengthening of Hamas-Iranian ties was 'Imad al-'Alami, a Hamas leader expelled from the territories in 1990 who became head of the Hamas information bureau in Tehran. Established in 1991, the bureau was bolstered by frequent visits of Hamas leaders there, and became an official channel of dialogue and coordination between Hamas and Iran. Still, this did not signal any essential change in the relationship between the two, which retained a low profile, despite numerous media reports on the subject. Similarly, relations between Hamas and Hizballah were low key, despite the permanent presence of Hamas representatives in Syria and Lebanon.[34] Although Hamas spokesmen emphasized unity in the common goal of the struggle against the conquest in South Lebanon and Palestine, they denied the existence of operative cooperation with Hizballah.[35]

A reserved stance toward the Shi'a; strong affinity to the Brothers movements in Egypt and Jordan; and good relations with the Gulf states, all constituted a brake on deepening ties with Iran or its protégé, Hizballah. Hamas' preferred policy was one of cautious and controlled cooperation rather than the acceptance of patronage. For Iran, this meant limited accessibility to Palestinian politics, although its anti-Israel fervor and the political capital it gained from Hizballah's success in forcing the IDF withdrawal from Lebanon (May 2000) served as a convenient camouflage for socioeconomic failures at home.

Chapter Six:
World of Images and Symbols

The Islamic Jihad's world of images, drawn essentially from the Iranian model, constitutes one of the important channels through which the movement seeks to extend and solidify its revolutionary messages. These messages aim to create a conceptual framework centering on Palestine and the need to liberate it through armed jihad. The linkage between ideological content and the expressive dimension, or idiom, in Sivan's analysis,[1] is reflected in the adoption of militaristic-religious terminology and the use of visual symbols. The power of linguistic references, that reflect longing for a glorious past and are charged with simplified religious terms, endows the movement's messages with vitality and legitimation. Language is capable of bringing people together or driving a wedge between them, and is thus an important agent of socialization and indoctrination; when used in a mythical way, it can evoke strong emotion.[2] In mapping the Islamic Jihad's world of symbols, the motif that stands out most conspicuously is that of the duty of jihad and martyrdom.

Peace, the Islamic Jihad holds, is the basis of Islam, and war is the exception. However, war is permissible in two situations: defense of soul, honor, property and homeland from an enemy; and defense of faith, in the event that someone seeks to curtail it by harming the preacher or the believer.[3] In the view of the movement, authorization for such a war is to be found in the portions of the Qur'an and the Hadith that deal with the heroic image of the Prophet. Wisely integrating the virtues of spiritual shepherd, statesman and military commander into his leadership, the Prophet also demonstrated the consistent application of the duty of jihad in his frequent conquests. Determination and patience in the clash between Islam and heresy tilted the balance of power in favor of Islam and converted believers from a persecuted minority in Mecca into an expansive nation.[4]

The movement's frequent references to the distant past are not merely anachronistic or apologetic, but serve as a source of inspiration for a better future. In many respects, the idealization of the past also means defying the present and challenging its values and premises. In this sense, the revival of the duty of jihad, which dominated Islam in its early days, is the only guarantee for the Muslims' complete victory over their enemies, especially in Palestine. There, the Zionist presence is likened to a cancerous growth that destroys the nation's body.[5] The reference, then, is to a restitutive jihad, based on a religio-historic sanction aimed at sustaining Muslim zeal and at bringing about a fundamental change in the status quo.

Since Israel embodies the essence of the Western offensive at the heart of the Muslim world, the struggle against it is obligatory for every believer who is sound in mind and body. The urgency of the issue also prohibits deferring jihad until the reestablishment of the caliphate or a large Islamic state outside Palestine, as the Liberation Party, for example, insists. While the Islamic Jihad emphasizes that Islam sets restrictions on acts permissible in war, and prohibits the killing of women, children and the aged, it justifies exceptions to these prohibitions for two reasons: Israel's racist policy against the Palestinians and its attacks on the sanctity of Islam; and the militaristic nature of Israeli society, which makes it difficult to differentiate between soldiers and ordinary citizens. One of the movement's publications termed Zionism the "twin brother" of German Nazism, and the struggle against it as a battle for survival. Coexistence was not an option.[6]

An uncompromising struggle with Israel represented a confrontation of identity and culture rather than of politics and geography. As such, it legitimized a variety of available means of fighting, and especially martyrdom (*istishhad*). The movement positioned martyrdom as the pinnacle of the worship of Allah and as the central criterion in determining man's fate for good or ill in the hereafter, namely, between a life of pleasure in paradise and torment in hell:

> The life of the present world is only ephemeral. However, it is the arena of struggle between faith and heresy; worship of God and worship of impulses and vanities. This is what turns life into a bridge by which to reach paradise, providing that man aspires to be a grateful servant of Allah, or a bridge to the fire of hell if he wants to estrange himself from Allah.[7]

Martyrdom is designed not only for the worship of Allah, but also to guarantee the existence of the community of believers. According to *al-Mujahid*, the martyr does not seek egotistic satisfaction but rather views acts on behalf of others as a duty. While he earns eternal life, his fellowmen on earth earn honorable lives.[8] Martyrdom does not conflict with Muslim commands that prohibit self-immolation or suicide (*intihar*). The Islamic Jihad strictly differentiates between martyrdom and self-immolation, positing the test of intention as the dividing line between them. A martyr is someone who strikes at the enemy on behalf of Allah and the faith, while a suicide damages his soul in order to end life out of despair, poverty or fear. The punishment for the latter is hell, inasmuch as Allah created man and breathed part of his soul into him.[9]

Responding to the charge that the act of jihad against the enemy in itself meant certain death, so that the act was in effect one of suicide, the movement holds that the call for jihad is inherently a call for sacrifice on behalf of Allah. The historic record of early Islam, the movement has pointed out, indicates the existence of three levels of encounter with the enemy: a situation in which either the death or the survival of the perpetrator are possible, in which case he will earn either eternal life or earthly honor; a situation in which death is likely, if the balance of power favors the enemy; and a situation in which death is certain, so the perpetrator goes to his death convinced that he will reach paradise. Other situations in which the believer is aware of the possibility that his act will cause his death are refusal to relinquish his religion or speak heresy, and the struggle against despotic rulers.[10]

The practical interpretation of martyrdom is frontal encounter with the enemy, which combines initial surprise with determination "until death for Allah." This can be implemented by carrying sabotage charges, driving a booby-trapped car, or penetrating with arms into public buildings. Such acts would ensure numerous losses by the enemy, demoralize its ranks and heighten the power of Islam. Neglect of jihad or hesitancy regarding martyrdom do not stem from legal equivocation, but rather reflect the condition of decline of the Muslim nation in modern times. They signify a violation of the Shari'a and a denial of the glorious heritage of the past.[11]

Another pattern of self-sacrifice is firm resolve in the face of interrogation and torture by the enemy security services, so as to deny them information about other members or weapons stores that could harm the movement. Physical victory on the battlefield is thereby paralleled by psychological victory during imprisonment, which will be achieved only if the fighter's body does not surrender under the pressure of captivity and torture.[12] The absence of material comfort in prison serves only to strengthen the spirit of the prisoner. A prime example was supplied by Shiqaqi, who recounted that during the tortures he underwent in an Israeli prison before his expulsion, he felt closer than ever to the moment of relinquishing his spirit for the sanctification of Allah.[13]

While the Islamic Jihad's strong affinity to Shi'i Iran and its delegitimation of Arab regimes left it with no significant strategic backing, its position on martyrdom gained wide support in Islamic circles, both official and oppositionist. Most of them justified and even encouraged the Palestinian suicide attacks. A *fatwa* issued in March 1996 by a group of Egyptian 'ulama' placed those who committed such attacks in the top rank of martyrdom. The shaykh of al-Azhar, Muhammad Sayyid Tantawi, the senior legal authority in the Sunni world, while asserting in September 1997 that Islam rejected all forms of violence, praised the suicide attacks in Palestine as "a type of legitimate defense."[14] This view was shared by spokesmen for the Islamic movements.

Shaykh Yusuf al-Qirdawi, one of the Muslim Brothers' main ideologists, held that martyrdom is the ammunition provided especially to the weak so that they can stand fast against despotism and heresy. While rejecting indiscriminate killing, he argued that Israel was a militaristic society, and if a child or an old person were killed, this was part of the risk inherent in such attacks; necessity was overriding. A similar argument was used by the Islamist writer Fahmi Huwaydi, who viewed the Palestinian Islamic attacks as "another page in the struggle between sacrifice and oppressor."[15]

Such statements by eminent 'ulama' and perceived moderate Islamists imply that the ideological barrier to domestic violence against a Muslim ruler (i.e., *fitna*) was readily removed in the case of Israel, which was denounced as heretical and targeted for defamation through all of Muslim historiography. While the Islamic Jihad did not require outside religious approval to justify violence against Israel, when this was given, it was used widely.[16]

The fostering of martyrdom was well reflected on three levels: the radical political myth, armed activity, and visual symbols and holidays.

The Radical Political Myth

In his book "Arab Political Myths," Emmanuel Sivan defines myth as a type of political allegory with a dramatic narrative that is founded on a true historic event. The factual nucleus of the event is reworked and expanded, and it acquires an epic significance. Myth serves two functions: an interpretive one—placing the current reality of a group or society in historical context and interpreting it in light of past experience; and an operative function—seeking to shape the conduct of the community and mobilize it for action aimed at consolidating or, alternatively, undermining the existing order. Since the myth is adapted to the historic circumstances that it seeks to interpret and mold, it is a dynamic device divested of its archaic status in time and place. Its importance lies in its appeal to the emotional rather than rational stratum of human experience. The myth, therefore, is a confirmed enemy of the mundane and the banal. It pushes aside the trivial and the ordinary, infusing the contemporary experience with cosmic, supra-historical significance.[17]

Two historic events in the Palestinian context have been elevated to the level of myth by the Islamic Jihad, whose heroes are identified with the struggle between liberation and enslavement: the Qassamist movement of the 1920s and 1930s, and the Shaja'iyya battle of 1987.

The movement defined Shaykh 'Izz al-Din al-Qassam as the most outstanding religious figure to have carried out jihad against Western imperialism and its allies in the region despite the oppressive circumstances under which he operated. Qassam, of Syrian origin, served as imam of the al-Istaqlal mosque in Haifa and led the resistance against both the British and the Jews in Palestine in the latter 1920s and early 1930s. The movement drew a parallel between the death of Qassam, in a clash with a British force in 1935, and that of Imam Husayn bin 'Ali in Karbala' (680) "as a unique human example of martyrdom for truth and justice." Like Husayn during the 7th century, "Qassam in the 20th century was a model of faith and revolution."[18] Descriptions of him put great emphasis on his dissident character vis-à-vis the traditional leadership under Hajj Amin al-Husayni, his concern for the poor and the weak in society, and his heroic death combating the forces of injustice.[19]

The Islamic Jihad rejected attempts over the years by Palestinian secular factions to blur the authentic identity of the Qassamite movement and ascribe a nationalist or social dimension to it. "Its true and legal successor," *al-Mujahid* claimed, is the Islamic Jihad, which emerged in the 1980s.[20] Symbols were provided in the form of the al-Qassam mosque in northern Gaza, a stronghold of the movement, and the organ *al-Istiqlal*, named for the mosque in Haifa in which Qassam had preached. In emphasizing its historic continuity with the Qassamite movement, the Islamic Jihad aimed to achieve two goals: gain recognition as an important element with historic roots in Palestine; and highlight the religious dimension in the Jewish-Arab conflict, which had been minimized by the predominance of the secular-nationalist narrative. The Islamization of the Qassamist episode was also evident in Hamas, whose military arm is named the al-Qassam Battalions. Thus, the historiographic dispute between Islamists and secular nationalists over the Qassamist legacy was integral part of the political struggle to shape Palestinian identity.

The movement's perpetuation of Qassam's legacy was exemplified in a series of successful attacks by six of its members after they escaped from the central Gaza prison in May 1987, which made a deep impression on the Palestinian public. The attacks climaxed in an armed confrontation with Israeli security forces in the Shaja'iyya quarter of Gaza (October 1987), during which four of the group were killed. The merit of the Shaja'iyya battle, in the movement's narrative, lay not only in its fulfilment of every Muslim fighter's wish to enjoy the pleasures of paradise, but also in that it paved the way for the Intifada.[21]

The Islamic Jihad's desire to establish the Shaja'iyya incident as a model for emulation is reflected in memorial days for the fallen, and the dissemination of leaflets and obituary articles calling for intensifying the struggle.[22] The politicization of the incident also involved the families of the dead. In an interview in *al-Mujahid* marking the fourth anniversary of the event, the mother of one of the slain heroes, Muhammad al-Jamal, highlighted the role of the Muslim woman in raising a generation of fighters who will carry on the struggle and thwart efforts for a political settlement.[23]

The advocation of martyrdom based on the Qassam and Shaja'iyya models was not limited to the mythic plane, but was applied by the Islamic Jihad operationally as well. This correlation between the rhetorical and practical dimensions consolidated the revolutionary message of the movement and allowed it to present itself as one of the pioneers of jihad in Palestine.

Armed Activity

An examination of the Islamic Jihad's armed activity reveals daring and commitment by its members in carrying out attacks against Israeli targets, both civilian and military. One example was a well-planned ambush of IDF soldiers in South Lebanon (April 1992), during which two soldiers were killed and five were wounded. Another was the prolonged self-fortification by a leader of the movement in the West Bank, 'Isam Barahima, in a house near Jenin, prompting a military siege by an Israeli force. Barhama managed to keep the force at bay for 12 hours, killing an Israeli officer, before the house was razed to its foundations and he was killed (December 1992). The crowning operations were the suicide bombings that followed the signing of the Oslo Accords and the establishment of the PA.[24] The suicide attacks executed by the Islamic Jihad (and even more so by Hamas) were a prime cause of public concern in Israel and the PA. They also served to test the credibility of Palestinian Islam. Most of the attacks were presented as revenge for criminal acts by Israel against the Palestinians or for the killing of Islamic activists.[25] They endowed the Islamic Jihad and Hamas with credibility in terms of the commitment to exact retribution for every act of provocation against the Palestinians.

The violent attacks carried out by the movement, which sometimes ended in the death of the perpetrators, cannot be depicted as blind fanaticism. They reflected revolutionary activism marked by a deep belief in jihad and martyrdom and the duty to implement them here and now. Their standard-bearers were generally young, inter alia because of the ardor of youth and the absence of the limitations of family, work or financial obligations. Their religious fervor was reflected in the "wills" left by the fallen members of the movement, which stressed their yearning for martyrdom in the hope of "meeting Allah."[26]

Immortalizing the martyrs, the movement went beyond publishing their photographs and composing obituaries. It organized mass conferences in their honor, extolling their legacy as a true reflection of the "unbreakable spirit of Islam." The mourners' reception areas in the homes of the families of martyrs turned into joyous support gatherings.[27]

Shiqaqi's death in October 1995 constituted a notable input in the ritualization of martyrdom, "without which there is no life, history or glory," as he himself had written.[28] The mythologization of his image

Funeral procession for an Islamic Jihad activist in Gaza.

included the depiction of him as born in the shadow of the Arab defeat of 1948 and sacrificing himself in the shadow of the Arab surrender to Israel and the West in 1995.

Ceremony marking the annual memorial day of the death of Fathi al-Shiqaqi, Nablus, November 1997.

Shiqaqi had projected himself as Qassam's successor in perceiving Islam as a religion of liberation from all forms of tyranny. According to *al-Istiqlal*, Shiqaqi "in life and in death was the new Qassam." The link between his murder and the murder of Israel's Prime Minister Rabin several weeks later (November 1995), moreover, was defined as a "decree from heaven," since it was Rabin, in his role as minister of defense, who had signed the deportation order against Shiqaqi in 1988. The movement's publications featured Shiqaqi's photograph surrounded by photographs of other members who were killed.[29]

Portrait of Fathi al-Shiqaqi, center, with Islamic Jihad martyrs.
The caption reads: The Commander and his Martyred Disciples Greet Allah.

This point leads to a discussion of the visual aspect, which has served the Islamic Jihad as a significant social medium, equal to that of the printed word or the deed in fostering dissent and martyrdom.

Visual Symbols and Holidays

The most obvious way to assess the visual aspect of the movement's projection of revolutionary activism is by exploring its published organs, *al-Mujahid* (Beirut) and *al-Istiqlal* (Gaza). Their cover pages have featured the motto "Allah akbar," a picture of the al-Aqsa mosque and a map of the whole of Palestine. The inside pages frequently run photographs and caricatures depicting resistance to the occupation, such as mass encounters with IDF forces, popular parades and bereaved mothers holding pictures of their slain loved ones.[30]

The Islamic Jihad logo

The attempt to mold a collective Palestinian identity in the spirit of Islam, moreover, was closely bound up with the Islamic calendar of holidays. As traditional foci of worship and social encounter, Islamic holidays and rituals could easily be turned into rallying points for political protest. Sivan aptly defines the political and social function of holidays by describing them as "a special bloc of time that is almost holy, cut off from 'regular' time, in which the primary ceremonies of the human collective are held. The holiday calendar organizes collective time and gives it rhythm."[31]

The politicization of Islamic holidays largely reflects the movement's dual strategy of *da'wa* and jihad. This duality is especially noticeable in the Ramadan fast. Side by side with the emphasis on the importance of fasting and giving charity as a means of "purifying the soul from the sins of the body," the movement in its leaflets terms Ramadan "the month of jihad and sacrifice" in which the early Muslims achieved their greatest victories.[32] Similarly, 'Id al-Fitr, which ends the Ramadan fast, is referred to as the "Holiday of the Martyrs" by the Islamic Jihad, during which the Palestinians are called upon to rebel against their oppressor.[33]

Another modern holiday that is given special emphasis because of the emotional and political tension it evokes is World Jerusalem Day (*Yawm al-Quds al-'Alami*), taken from the Iranian calendar, which falls on the last Friday of Ramadan. Having become an important component in the political mythology of Iran, this holiday is marked by the Islamic Jihad and its sister Shi'i movements in Lebanon by symbolic military marches and popular parades. The central motif of this holiday is the holiness of Jerusalem to Islam and the need to liberate it from the defilement of the Jewish grip.[34]

Another element of the Islamic Jihad calendar is memorial days, which may be classified in three categories: the commemoration of historic events marking Islam's victory over its enemies; the remembrance of traumatic events in modern Palestinian history; and days of solidarity with the martyrs and detainees of the movement.[35] The mixture of heroic victories side by side with tragic defeats and mourning, elicits frustration but also anticipation for a better future for the believers. People are called upon on these memorial days to engage in violent activity against the IDF, to display civil disobedience such as commercial strikes, and to refrain from going to work in Israel.

Leaflets, a key Palestinian device to articulate values, define goals and evoke an active response by the public,[36] is doubly useful in the case of the Islamic Jihad. Unlike the PLO/PA and Hamas, which profit from an effective presence in Palestinian society, the Islamic Jihad's center of gravity is located outside the territories. The leaflets, therefore, constitute a vehicle for imparting messages and guiding collective behavior. They convey the movement's authority and help preserve its political status. The texts of the leaflets, like those of Hamas, are composed in an emotional language that makes extensive use of images laden with religious fervor. The current reality in Palestine is portrayed in absolute terms as a fateful struggle between right and heresy, and Palestinians are exhorted to use their spiritual resources to the utmost in order to rout Israeli injustice. The concluding motif of most of the leaflets projects the activist spirit of the Islamic Jihad: "Glory and eternity to the martyrs of our people...Long live Arab Islamic Palestine, liberated from the sea to the river."[37]

Conclusion

Up until the outbreak of the Intifada in December 1987, the religious resurgence that had overtaken the Middle East from the early 1970s onward seemed to have passed over Palestine, leaving hegemony there in the hands of Palestinian nationalism and its exponent, the PLO. However, the Islamic imprint on the events of the Intifada revealed the depth of Islam's hold on Palestinian society and confirmed its vitality as a cultural as well as political force.

The Islamic Jihad, which emerged in the early 1980s in the Gaza Strip, played a key role in molding radical Islam and establishing it as a legitimate form of struggle against Israel. Its main features were in two interrelated areas: ideological, in blending politics with violence; and social, in constituting a young, educated leadership cadre from the lower stratum dedicated to changing reality by revolutionary means.

The noted Islamist writer, Tawfiq al-Tayyib, sketching a normative profile of the modern Islamic movement, cited these attributes: a movement inspired by divine rather than positivist commandment and viewing earthly life as a bridge to the next world; a movement that respects human intellect for understanding divine revelation, yet is also aware of its limitations since revelation represents the absolute truth; a movement that allows room for personal freedom but does not view it as indispensable; and a movement that promotes governance by ethical values and views faith as a means for social change and not only as a set of rituals.[1] This profile largely applies to the Islamic Jihad both in terms of its ideological platform and in its patterns of activity.

The conversion of Islam into a theology of liberation, together with a series of successful violent attacks during 1986–87, imparted significant prestige to the Islamic Jihad. It forced the two major actors in Palestinian politics, the PLO and the Brothers, onto the defensive. In response, the PLO attempted to ride the wave of religious fervor by establishing the Islamic Fatah in the mid-1980s, while the Brothers established Hamas as their activist arm on the eve of the Intifada. This response, together with a firm Israeli policy (widespread arrests and the deportation of leaders), led to a significant erosion in the Islamic Jihad's standing in the territories and caused it to shift its focus of activity to the Arab diaspora. The existence of an infrastructure outside the territories, especially in Syria and Lebanon, largely subordinated the movement to dependence on the favors of the host regimes in its struggle against Israel.

In essence, the Islamic Jihad's political discourse sanctified a universal perception of Islam that posited the goals of removing the threat of the West and unifying the Muslim world. However, the emphasis on the liberation of Palestine and the focus of activity within its geographic boundaries turned the broader message into a territorial one imbued with specific Palestinian content. The case of the Islamic Jihad, as that of other Islamic movements in the Middle East, reflected the adaptation of Islamic thought to the 20th century reality of geographic divisions and separate political entities.[2] This adaptation was well entrenched in the agenda of Islamists, which focused on enhancing the Islamic character of the Arab polities, mainly through the enforcement of the Shari'a, rather than challenging their territorial boundaries and restoring the caliphate. The pan-Islamic idea, while preserved, was postponed to a distant future. Incorporating national identity into the Islamist discourse, however, also meant subordinating its legitimacy to a religious source.

In the Palestinian context, the Islamic Jihad did not disqualify patriotism or nationalism (*wataniyya*) so long as these were aimed at defending the land and the rights of its people, and therefore sanctified by Islam. But if loyalty to the land takes ascendancy over Islam, the movement held, this became heresy and must be opposed. Defining the unique position of Palestine in the cultural conflict waged by Muslims against their enemies, Shiqaqi stated that "we were in no way a connecting link between Islam and nationalism, but a thread interwoven between the absolute truth and history, from the Qur'an to Palestine."[3] A similar position was articulated in Hamas' 1988 charter.[4]

The Islamic Jihad's perception of Palestine in religious terms seems to echo the political biographies of its leaders, which contain no trace of activity in the PLO. On the contrary, most of these young academics had operated within existing Islamic movements, especially in the Brothers and the Liberation Party, until the rise of radical Islam in the territories. This fact distinguished the movement from the other jihad factions, which were linked both ideologically and organizationally with Fatah, and explains its alienation from the essentially secular premise of Palestinian nationalism.

Its rejection of the nationalist perception, however, did not prevent the Islamic Jihad from cooperating with the PLO, so long as the latter adhered to its commitment to armed struggle. This readiness was sustained during the Intifada. By then, however, its focus had shifted from Fatah, which opted for a historical compromise with Israel, to the Palestinian left, which remained loyal to the strategy of armed resistance. At the opposite pole, the appearance of Hamas as a reflection of change in the Brothers' approach to the jihad in Palestine fostered a positive dialogue between it and the Islamic Jihad.

Relations between the Islamic and leftist forces—formalized with the establishment of the Ten Palestinian Factions and, thereafter, the Palestinian Alliance Forces—never progressed beyond the declarative level. These two oppositionist forums, lacking any real political capabilities, proved to be restricted and peripheral. The main reasons were not only differences over the future nature of the Palestinian polity, but also attempts by Hamas to use the opposition in undermining the PLO's status. The two leading leftist factions, the DFLP and PFLP, while not concealing their disdain for 'Arafat, were far from ready to dismantle the PLO. Eventually, they were forced out of the Alliance as a result of their willingness to engage in dialogue with the PA. The DFLP even publicly declared its support for a two-state solution in Palestine,[5] thereby further aggravating the fragile position of the opposition camp.

Moreover, efforts by the Islamic opposition to promote harmony within its own ranks met with little success. The main obstacles were the historic animosity between the Islamic Jihad and Hamas' progenitor, the Brothers; the disdainful attitude displayed by Hamas, as the leading Islamic force in the territories, toward its partners; and improved relations between Tehran and Hamas, which relegated the Islamic Jihad to a secondary position in the context of the relationship with Iran. In addition, the Islamic Jihad's delegitimation of most of the Arab regimes left it, in contrast to Hamas, with few patrons in the Arab world—namely, Syria, Lebanon and Sudan, Iran's main allies in the region. This fact endowed the movement with ideological credibility, but perpetuated its inferior status in Palestinian politics, an inferiority reinforced in the wake of the Oslo Accords.

The Oslo Accords, followed by the establishment of the Palestinian Authority, shifted the PLO's role from a resistance movement to the guardian of a state-in-formation. The civil infrastructure that had developed in the Gaza Strip and the West Bank after 1967 could have served 'Arafat in building up a living, modern Palestinian polity. Yet he chose to neutralize this force and eliminate any type of political opposition, secular or Islamic. His justification was the objective of state-building, which, he claimed, required political stability through a strong central authority. As Sara Roy put it, "'Arafat's agenda was survival rather than democracy."[6] This rationale also determined the stance of the PA toward the Islamic opposition.

From the start, the PA set out to reduce the strength of the Islamic opposition and its standard-bearer, Hamas, both through co-option and through political and physical pressure. These measures, however, did not reach the level of violent confrontation: 'Arafat was aware of the strong Islamic sentiment in society, and he needed maximal local support in the peace talks with Israel. The intent, rather, was essentially to redefine the boundaries of legitimate activity for Islamists in light of the presence of a central authority. In this sense, the rivalry between the PA and the Islamists gradually assumed the nature of a struggle between regime and opposition along the same lines as in the Arab countries. Deviation from the rules of the political game dictated by the PA was met by preventive arrests, swifts trials and closures of institutions.

This reality prompted Islamic Jihad and Hamas to reach a modus vivendi with the PA not formalized in any binding agreement. Such an adaptation could preserve Islamist civil assets, yet also defuse the clash between ideological dogma and political adjustment, especially on the issue of armed struggle against Israel. The guideline for both Hamas and the Islamic Jihad was avoidance of confrontation with the PA, in recognition of its superior power; and an emphasis on promoting democracy in society. In advocating democracy, the two movements were aided by the Palestinians' grievances toward the PA, which, while acknowledged as a legitimate authority, was criticized for its endemic corruption and constant violation of human rights.[7]

The Islamic Jihad's proclivity for ideological premises, however, was greater than that of Hamas, due to its elitist nature and its limited influence. By contrast, Hamas established itself as a popular movement, whose primary strength lay in communal rather than military activity. In essence, Hamas retained the Brothers' long-term strategy of Islamization from the bottom up, despite its continued armed struggle against Israel. This enabled Hamas to position itself as a significant rival to the PLO during the Intifada, and as the main opposition to the PA during the peace process. Evidence of the movement's reformist orientation was the relative flexibility displayed by "inside" leaders toward the PA, as well as the appearance of rifts in its ranks. While Hamas' entrenched position and ideological affinity to the Brothers allowed it greater maneuverability between jihad and *da'wa*, without straying from the basic conception of the struggle in Palestine, the Islamic Jihad adhered essentially to jihad. This was expressed clearly in its internal charter (see Appendix), which cited armed jihad against Israel as the primary goal and communal activity as a secondary aspect. The terminology most widely used by the movement's spokesmen was "Islamization of society" by means of confrontation with the enemy (*al-tarbiyya bil-saddam.*).[8]

Jihad had been the Islamic Jihad's first strategic choice prior to the Intifada. It became an even more immediate need in the wake of the Oslo Accords. This emphasis exposed the movement to heightened repression by the PA, which also exploited the Islamic Jihad's rivalry with other Jihad factions to undermine the movement's status. As a consequence, Ramadan Shalah described the PA-Islamic Jihad relationship as one of "oppressor and oppressed."[9]

The modus vivendi between Hamas and the PA was also fragile, especially in the wake of the series of fatal attacks against Israel during February–March 1996. Yet, Hamas' broad civil network and its frequent contacts with PA representatives allowed it latitude. Hamas leaders argued that the main enemy was the occupation, although they pointed out that dialogue with the PA is "a means only, and means change, while rights are permanent."[10] Hamas' agenda, inspired by the Brothers' reformist outlook in the Middle East, especially in Egypt and Jordan, also dictated a greater degree of adaptation to the new reality created by the Oslo Accords.

In examining the Islamic opposition's ability to serve as a counterweight to the PLO in the struggle over the image of Palestinian society, the question arises as to its capacity to reconcile ideological outlook with political reality. By insisting on a prolonged, tenacious struggle with Israel until its total rout, the Islamic opposition seemed to be unable to provide a concrete solution to the distress of the Palestinians. Some scholars believed that in the inhospitable circumstances induced by the peace process, Islamic politics were unable to influence developments in the arena of the conflict. Alternatively, however, its forces might develop a tendency toward moderation that would of necessity lead it to integrate into the new political order.[11] Against these arguments, one may note, first, that the cornerstone of the Oslo Accords was the security component, which was also its Achilles heel, as the attacks of February–March 1996 proved; these attacks played a significant role in the ascent to power of a rightist government in Israel in June 1996. Second, while the existence of a political entity with coercive power compelled Palestinian Islamists to reassess their modes of operation, this implied political realism rather than ideological moderation or strategic change in the vision itself. That vision continued to call for both the Islamization of society and the complete liberation of Palestine. Defined sociologically, Hamas and the Islamic Jihad may be described as value-oriented movements[12] divested of sectorial overtones and striving in the name of an inclusive belief system—Islam—for a radical change in society. This change was projected as requiring a "long breath" (*sabr*), but its results were preordained. In the words of the Egyptian Islamist Shaykh Yusuf al-Qirdawi, "patience is an earthly necessity as well as a religious one. There is no success in this world or in the other without patience."[13]

Significantly, religious fervor regarding Israel and the application of the Shari'a continued to imbue those Islamists, mostly from Hamas, who had joined PA bodies on a personal basis or through political parties. Shaykh Hamid al-Bitawi, head of the Shari'a courts in the West Bank, for example, warned against cooperating with Jews in light of their deceitfulness and voiced alarm over the decline in religious morals under the PA. The Salvation Party asserted in its platform that "Islam is a method of government encompassing all areas of life, and is the convincing answer to our problems in the modern era." Its political agenda was well defined by its leader, Yahya Musa, who stated that "the party's first priority is to liberate the individual before liberating the land. Its aim is to shape social behavior based on equality and justice as a complement to liberation."[14] Although these Islamic elements accepted the new political order in the territories, they sought to inject metaphysical values into it. This goal was also shared by the religious establishment, who adopted an assertive stance on the preservation of the Islamic ethos in society.[15]

According to Shaykh 'Akrama Sabri, the Mufti of Palestine, "every nation has its own values and habits. What is permitted and fitting in America, is not permitted or fitting in our country."[16]

Alarmed by the "theft of holy land" and the danger of the Middle East turning into a "Zionist region," the Islamic Jihad and Hamas sought to expose the fragility of the Oslo Accords. To do so they employed violent means (military attacks) and nonviolent methods (political struggle over civil power bases, and foiling normalization, *tatbi'*). While armed struggle continued to serve as a central pillar in their platform, in practice it was subordinated to constraints stemming from increasingly harsh treatment by the PA. However, the dissident stance of both movements in their rejection of the Oslo Accords made their conflict with the PA a central feature of Palestinian politics.

The two sides represented two opposing world views—one seeking to advance limited, attainable goals in a given reality, the other embracing the past and fashioning a world of unequivocal injunctions. In political terms, the latter perception was forced onto the defensive. Gradually, in the wake of a series of violent clashes, its spokesmen came to realize what other Islamic movements in the Middle East had learned, that in facing a regime with coercive powers, dialogue was preferable to confrontation in order to avoid grave political and organizational damage. While the harmony with the national camp that was emphasized in the charters of both Hamas and the Islamic Jihad was not achieved, escalation of the friction to widespread bloodshed did not occur either.

A source of encouragement to Palestinian Islamists was the strong religious and anti-Israeli sentiment in society, fueled by chronic socioeconomic distress, especially in the refugee camps. As one Hamas leader put it: "Hatred of the conquerors is a part of the mental structure of the Palestinians and this prompts them to continue their struggle."[17] The predominance of Islam in society prevented the PA from mounting an all-out war against the Islamic movements. This was especially so regarding Hamas, which controlled a large network of charitable associations that provided vital welfare services to a large needy community. Hamas' philanthropic work was backed by such financial bodies as the Bayt al-Mal investment firm, established in East Jerusalem in 1994, and the Al-Aqsa Bank opened in Ramallah in 1999. The PA did not hide its disapproval of the link between the existence of an autonomous civil network and a dissident political force, and even drafted a restrictive bill in 1995 to strengthen its authority over NGOs. However, the Authority's meager resources, and its reluctance to antagonize local and world public opinion, allowed for the relatively smooth functioning of these institutions, which, according to World Bank data in 1996, numbered approximately 1,200.[18]

Another source of encouragement to Palestinian Islamists was the fragility of the Israeli-Egyptian and Israeli-Jordanian peace, each of which remained largely a peace between governments rather than peoples. While the Islamic Jihad and Hamas acknowledged that the expansion of peace in the region to such important countries as Syria, Lebanon and the Gulf states would have a negative effect on the struggle in Palestine, they pledged that this would not terminate their activity. According to Shiqaqi, the struggle in Israel was multifaceted and determined by variables of time and place, but these did not entail a truce. In Palestine, the emphasis would be on armed jihad; in Egypt on political activity; and elsewhere on cultural and social action. Comprehensive peace, he declared, also meant widening the arena of confrontation with Israel and entrusting it to the hands of the Arab and Muslim peoples. In contrast to their rulers, the people viewed Palestine as holy land and rejected any normalization with Israel. As the experience in Egypt and Jordan had shown, the people were motivated by deeply religious faith and a natural aspiration for freedom and progress, a goal conditional upon ongoing resistance to Israel.[19]

The Islamic Jihad argued that any peace arrangement to be concluded in the region will be based on an oppressive balance of power, and as such it will be temporary and fragile. This will conform to the course of history, which is moving toward a shift in the world balance of power in favor of Islam.[20] In emphasizing historical determinism, which promises ultimate victory to the Muslims, the Islamic Jihad and Hamas sought to ratify the "long breath" policy in the struggle with Israel so as to sanction sustained sacrifice by the Palestinians.

Foiling normalization as the key to combating Israel and its expansionist scheme in the region became a central concept in Islamic discourse in the Middle East, especially after the Gulf War and the accelerated peace process of the early 1990s. This objective was also shared by the adversaries of the Islamists in the political and intellectual communities in the

Arab world, who played an important role in directing public opinion against Israel. While recognizing Israel's right to exist in peace, these Westernized secular elements rejected the integration of Israel into the regional system, dismissing the vision of the "new Middle East" as merely a lever to achieve Israeli dominance.

Among the Islamists, the outstanding expositor on the issue of normalization was Muhammad Husayn Fadlallah, the spiritual leader of Hizballah, who warned in 1993 that the danger to be anticipated from Israel in peacetime was no less than the danger from it during war. The task of the Islamic movements, he said, was to avoid an all-out confrontation with the local regimes, while preserving their right to address the people on religious and political issues.[21] In the Palestinian context, shifting the emphasis from armed jihad to communal activity, as dictated by circumstances, would not mean halting the struggle against Israel but rather continuing it by other means.

Indeed, the peace process between the PA and Israel following the signing of the Oslo Accords in 1993 proved to be delicate and fragile, witnessing setbacks that culminated in the eruption of violent clashes in September 2000 (dubbed the "al-Aqsa Intifada"). Ironically, the hardest hour for the Islamic opposition, which occurred while the final status talks over Palestine took place, turned into its hour of glory. The Arab-Israeli conflict, which had long been depicted in national-geographic terms, reverted to its original Muslim-Jewish nature, with a focus on al-Aqsa and the control over it. The events of the second Intifada reinstated the relevance of the Islamic narrative regarding the conflict in Palestine, creating points of coalescence with the national narrative on such loaded issues as Jerusalem and the right of the return of the refugees. As a result, the PA was constricted in its negotiations with Israel.

Moreover, the PA found itself in a sensitive situation vis-à-vis the Palestinian public. Its status as a sovereign entity in the territories had made it the address for the Palestinians' national aspirations but also for their daily grievances. Its poor civic performance, and the chronic corruption in its ranks, especially in light of the economic distress created by the al-Aqsa Intifada, exposed the Authority to mounting public criticism.

The bloody events in the territories and the sense of unity they evoked among the Palestinian factions did not blur the differences in outlook between the PA and the Islamists regarding the aims of the al-Aqsa

Intifada. While the PA viewed the Intifada as a political lever for reaching a better agreement with Israel, the Islamists regarded it as a return to the overall strategy of popular and armed struggle.[22] Reinforcement for this view was perceived by the Islamists in the supportive demonstrations throughout the Arab world, which were held up as an explicit political expression of opposition to peace with Israel. According to the Islamic Jihad, the al-Aqsa Intifada introduced public opinion as a major political factor that the Arab dictatorial regimes could not ignore. By positing the Arab public as the sole arbiter of the fate of Palestine, the Islamic Jihad in effect delegitimized the Arab leadership.[23] Hamas, too, praised the popular Arab stance as the strategic depth of the Intifada, but refrained from condemning the Arab regimes. It limited itself to the demand that they break off all diplomatic or economic contacts with Israel.[24] Another reinforcement for the Islamists' strategy of armed struggle in Palestine was the Lebanese case. The prolonged bloodletting of IDF soldiers there, they argued, exposed the breaking point of Israeli society and forced the Israeli government to withdraw from South Lebanon without concessions by the authorities in Beirut or by Hizballah.[25]

The dispute between the PA and the Islamists over the nature of the Intifada was in effect bound up with the broader struggle over the nature of Palestinian society. Each side posited a separate sociopolitical platform in which Israel constituted an important, though not exclusive, component. Ultimately, however, the superior political status of the PA as the sovereign body in the territories allowed it to dictate the Palestinian agenda, thus relegating the Islamic opposition to the status of respondent rather than initiator.

The transition of the PLO from a liberation movement to an evolving state granted Palestinian nationalism a territorial base and a governmental apparatus. It thereby put the PLO to the political test of attaining complete and genuine independence and economic well-being. The extent of its success in this test will also determine the vigor of the ideological antithesis, represented by political Islam.

NOTES

Abbreviations

The following abbreviations are used throughout the notes and bibliography.

DR   *Daily Report: Near East and South Asia* (Washington)
EI²   *Encyclopaedia of Islam,* 2nd edition (Leiden)
IJMES   *International Journal of Middle East Studies* (Cambridge)
MECS   *Middle East Contemporary Survey* (Boulder, Colorado)
MEJ   *Middle East Journal* (Washington)
MES   *Middle Eastern Studies* (London)

Preface

1. Emmanuel Sivan, *Radical Islam* (New Haven, 1985), p. 3.
2. William E. Shepard, "Islam and Ideology: Towards a Typology," *IJMES* (August 1987), pp. 308–9, 314–15; Donald E. Smith, *Religion and Political Development* (Boston, 1970), pp. 45–50, 60, 65–68; Muhammad al-Ghazali, *Min Huna Na'lamu* (5th edition, Cairo, n.d.), pp. 51–57. See also Daniel Pipes, *In the Path of God: Islam and Political Power* (New York, 1983), pp. 3–11, 29–47.
3. Shepard, pp. 308–9, 311–13.
4. For literature on millennialism and politics, see e.g., Michael Barkun, *Disaster and Millenium* (New Haven, 1974); Sylvia L. Thrupp (ed.), *Millennial Dreams in Action* (New York, 1970); Aviezer Ravitzky, *Freedom Inscribed* (Hebrew; Tel Aviv, 1999), pp. 92–102.
5. For literature on political Islam in the Middle East, definitions and characteristics, see Ali E. Dessouki, "The Islamic Resurgence, Sources, Dynamics and Implications," in idem. (ed.), *Islamic Resurgence in the Arab World* (New York, 1982), pp. 3–9; Saad Eddin Ibrahim, "Anatomy of Egypt's Islamic Groups: Methodological Note and Preliminary Findings," *IJMES* (1980), Vol. 12, pp. 423–53; Hava Lazarus-Yafeh, "Contemporary Fundamentalism, Judaism, Christianity, Islam," *The Jerusalem Quarterly*, No. 47 (Summer 1988), pp. 27–39.
6. The use of Islam as a vehicle to promote national goals was also evident as far back as the British Mandate period, when the urban notables headed by Hajj Amin al-Husayni opposed the Zionist threat. See, e.g., Uri M. Kupferschmidt, *The Supreme Muslim Council: Islam under the British Mandate for Palestine* (Leiden, 1987), pp. 228–47, 253–54.
7. For literature on Islamic Jihad, see Reuven Paz [M.A degree], *The Evolution of Islamic Palestinian Factors between 1967–1988* (Hebrew; Haifa, 1988), pp. 63–114; Robert Satloff, "Islam in the Palestinian Uprising," *Orbis*, No. 33 (Summer 1989),

pp. 393–95; Elie Rekhess, "The Iranian Impact on the Islamic Jihad Movement in the Gaza Strip," in David Menashri (ed.), *The Iranian Revolution and the Muslim World* (Boulder, 1990), pp. 190–206; Thomas Mayer, "Pro-Iranian Fundamentalism in Gaza," in Emmanuel Sivan and Menachem Friedman (eds.), *Religious Radicalism and Politics in the Middle East* (Albany, 1990), pp. 143–55; Jean Francois Legrain, "The Islamic Movement and the Intifada," in Jamal R. Sannar and Roger Heacock (eds.), *Intifada: Palestine at the Crossroads* (New York, 1990), pp. 176–81; Abdulaziz I. Zamel [M.A. degree], *The Rise of Palestinian Islamic Groups* (Tampa, 1991), pp. 183–211; Ziad Abu 'Amr, *Islamic Fundamentalism in the West Bank and Gaza Strip* (Bloomington, 1994), pp. 90–127; Meir Hatina, "Iran and the Palestinian Islamic Movement," *Orient*, Vol. 38, No. 1 (1997), pp. 107–13.

Introduction

1. On the rise of radical Islam and its ideological roots, see Sivan, pp. 16–49; Fouad Ajami, *The Arab Predicament* (Cambridge, 1981), pp. 50–63.
2. Cited in Sivan, p. 20 from the book written by 'Abd al-Salam Faraj, *al-Farida al-Gha'iba* (Cairo, 1982), p. 23.
3. On the Arab defeat in 1967 and its implications for Palestinian Islam, see Paz, pp. 64–71.
4. Abu 'Amr, pp. 91–92. In August 1992, Ya'qub Qarsh and Layth Shubaylat, both Islamist delegates in the Jordanian Parliament, were linked to an underground radical Islamic group affiliated with Iran and Ahmad Jibril's Popular Front—General Command. They were tried and sentenced to 20 years imprisonment, but later released as part of a general amnesty issued by King Husayn. *Ha'aretz*, 9 September 1992; *Filastin al-Muslima* (London), December 1992.
5. On the strengthening of the PLO's position in the territories, see Moshe Ma'oz, *The Palestinian Leadership in the West Bank* (Tel Aviv, 1985), pp. 129–32.
6. For the activities of the Supreme Muslim Council, see Sa'd al-Din al-'Alami, *Watha'iq al-Hayha al-Islamiyya al-'Ulya 1967–1984* (Jerusalem, 1984); Paz, pp. 46–51.
7. For the Brothers in the West Bank and Gaza before 1967, see Abu 'Amr, pp. 1–10; Rab'i al-Madhun, "al-Haraka al-Islamiyya fi Filastin," *Shu'un Filastiniyya*, No. 187 (October 1988), pp. 15–24; see also, Muhammad K. Shadid, "The Muslim Brotherhood Movement in the West Bank and Gaza," *Third World Quarterly*, April 1988, pp. 658–62.
8. For the activities of the Brothers in the 1970s, see Ahmad bin Yusuf (ed.), *Hamas Hadath 'Abir am Badil Da'im* (n.p, 1990), pp. 73–105; Zamel, pp. 24–36.
9. Munir Fasheh, "Political Islam in the West Bank," *Merip Reports*, No. 103 (February 1982), p. 16; Michel Jubran and Laura Drake, "The Islamist Fundamentalist Movement in the West Bank and Gaza Strip," *Middle East Policy*, Vol. 2, No. 2

(1993), pp. 4–5; Beverly Milton-Edwards, *Islamic Politics in Palestine* (London, 1996), pp. 106–8.

10. Cited by 'Abd al-Qadir Yasin, "Mawqi' Hamas fi al-Zahira al-Islamiyya fi al-Daffa wal-Qita'," *al-Urdunn al-Jadid*, Autumn 1988, p. 47.

11. For the Liberation Party and its ideological platform, see Taqi al-Din al-Nabhani, *Nizam al-Islam* (2nd edition, Jerusalem, 1953), pp. 43–44, 76–82; *al-Shira'* (Beirut), No. 4, 1984, pp. 20–23; Amnon Cohen, *Political Parties in the West Bank under the Jordanian Regime 1949–1967* (London, 1982), pp. 209–29. From the early 1980s, when the peace process first began to gather momentum, the Liberation Party increased its emphasis on the Palestinian issue and even called for the eradication of Israel by jihad. This, however, reflected the party's desire to win political credibility in the Palestinian arena rather than a departure from its basic ideological outlook—the installation of a caliph, who would then lead the jihad against the Jews. See *Afkar Siyasiyya li-Hizb al-Tahrir* (Beirut, 1994); Suha Taji-Farouki, "Islamists and the Threat of Jihad: Hizb al-Tahrir and the al-Muhajiroun on Israel and the Jews," *MES*, Vol. 36, No. 4 (October 2000), pp. 24–30.

12. Among these groups were *al-Salafiyyun* (Followers of the Pious Ancestors), based in Khan Yunis and led by Shaykh Salim Shurab; *al-Takfir wal-Hijra* (Atonement and Holy Flight), based in the Burayj refugee camp in the Gaza Strip, with branches in Jenin and Nablus; and *Rijal al-Da'wa* (Men of Preaching), based in several villages in the Bethlehem and Hebron areas. See Israeli Civil Administration publications, *Gaza Strip—Political Profile* (Hebrew; April 1986), pp. 42–43; *Islamic Activity in the West Bank* (Hebrew; April 1988), pp. 41–44; Shalom Cohen, "Khomeinism in Gaza," *New Outlook* (March 1980), pp. 6–9.

13. On the PLO policy of controlled radicalism, see Shaul Mishal and Reuben Aharoni, *Speaking Stones: Communiqués from the Intifada Underground* (New York, 1994), pp. 13–14.

14. On the emergence of radical Islam in the territories, see Hala Mustafa, "al-Tayyar al-Islami fi al-Ard al-Muhtalla," *al-Mustaqbal al-'Arabi* (July 1988), pp. 81–84; Madhun, pp. 27–28; Emile Sahliyeh, *In Search of Leadership: West Bank Politics since 1967* (Washington, D.C., 1988), pp. 139–44; Robert Satloff, "Islam in the Palestinian Uprising," *Orbis*, No. 33 (Summer 1989), pp. 391–92.

15. 'Umar al-Hufash and Khalid 'Awad, *Mub'adu Marj al-Zuhur* (Jerusalem, 1994), pp. 15–28; Sahliyeh, p. 46.

16. *Al-Sabil* (Oslo), 5 May 1989, p. 3.

Chapter One

1. One of the initiators of radical Islam in Egypt was Salah Sariyya, leader of *Shabab Muhammad*. This organization, founded in the early 1970s, was responsible for the attack on the Technical College in Cairo in April 1974. Sariyya was executed

by the Egyptian authorities in October 1975. He is considered one of the fathers of the Palestinian Jihad, as he himself was a Palestinian who was active in the PLO and later became a Muslim radical. On the ideological platforms of the Islamic militant groups in Egypt, see Israel Altman, "Islamic Movements in Egypt," *The Jerusalem Quarterly*, Vol. 10 (Winter 1979), pp. 97–104.

2. For biographical details on Shiqaqi, see Rif'at Sayyid Ahmad (ed.), *Rihlat al-Damm alladhi Hazama al-Sayf* (Cairo, 1996), Vol. I, pp. 47–50; Shiqaqi's interview in *al-Sharq al-Awsat*, 17 March 1995; Shiqaqi, "5 Huzayran," *al-Liwa*, 5 June 1991.

3. Sayyid Ahmad, Vol. I, p. 50; 'Izz al-Din al-Faris (hereafter: Shiqaqi), "Ma'alim fi al-Tariq," *al-Mukhtar al-Islami*, April 1981, pp. 74–90.

4. Sayyid Ahmad, Vol. 1, p. 51.

5. Ibid., pp. 51–52; Muhammad Muru, *Fathi al-Shiqaqi* (Cairo, 1997), pp. 3–6.

6. Ahmad Sadiq (hereafter, Bashir Nafi'), "Tahawi al-'Askar wa-Budhur al-Madd al-Islami," *al-Mukhtar al-Islami*, May 1981, pp. 40–48; Zamel, p. 187.

7. Muru, pp. 6–8, 11; Sayyid Ahmad, Vol. 1, pp. 52–53; Shiqaqi, *al-Khumayni al-Hall al-Islami wal-Badil* (Cairo, 1979).

8. Muru, p. 11; Sayyid Ahmad, Vol. 1, pp. 52–53; *al-Qalam*, January 1997; *al-Mukhtar al-Islami*, January 1987, p. 95. See also Mayer, pp. 143–44, 148.

9. Muru, pp. 12–13; Nafi' in *al-Mukhtar al-Islami*, May 1981, pp. 28–30; Shiqaqi, "Fi Dhikra Istishhad Khalid al-Islambuli," in Sayyid Ahmad, Vol. 1, pp. 624–625; *al-Nur*, 15 May 1982, pp. 2–5.

10. Muru, pp. 12–13.

11. Abu 'Amr, pp. 93–94; *Kayhan al-'Arabi* (Tehran), 15 February 1988; Rekhess, pp. 196–197.

12. Shiqaqi's interview in *al-Khalij* (Abu Dhabi), 27 August 1989.

13. Shiqaqi's interviews in: *al-Wahda* (Beirut), November 1992; *al-Watan* (Kuwait), 1 October 1994. The socio-demographic change in the religious leadership of the territories after 1967 was present in the Brothers as well. The establishment of Hamas and its integration into the Intifada, largely reflected the growing status of the young generation, such as Khalil Ibrahim al-Quqa, Mahmud al-Zahhar and 'Abd al-'Aziz al-Rantisi in the Gaza Strip, and Bassam Jarar, Jamal Salim and Jamal Mansur in the West Bank. See 'Ali al-Jarbawi, *al-Intifada wal-Qiyadat al-Siyasiyya fi al-Daffa al-Gharbiyya wa-Qita' Ghazza* (Beirut, 1989), pp. 48–51.

14. Bashir Nafi', "Ma'rifat al-Rijal bi al-Haqq am al-Haqq bi al-Rijal," *al-Tali'a al-Islamiyya*, January 1983, pp. 32–33.

15. Shiqaqi, *al-Khumayni*, pp. 38–39; *al-Mashru' al-Islami al-Mu'asir fi Filastin* (n.p., 1995), pp. 1–2; *al-Mujahid* (Beirut), 3 November 1989, pp. 1–2. See also 'Awda's interview in *al-Umma* (Beirut), December 1992.

16. Shiqaqi's interview in *al-Khalij*, 27 August 1989; Shiqaqi and Nafi', "al-Qadiyya al-Filastiniyya hiyya al-Qadiyya al-Markaziyya lil-Haraka al-Islamiyya," *al-Mukhtar al-Islami*, July 1980, pp. 31–35. This article was circulated in the territories as a booklet under the title *al-Qadiyya al-Filastiniyya min Manzur Islami*.

17. *Al-Mukhtar al-Islami*, June 1987, pp. 64–66; Shiqaqi's interview in *al-Wahda al-Islamiyya* (Beirut), 9 September 1988.

18. 'Awda's sermons appeared later in *al-Mujahid*, the movement organ published in Beirut. See, e.g., *al-Mujahid*, 22 February, 26 April 1991.

19. *Masirat al-Jihad al-Islami fi Filastin* (Beirut, 1989), pp. 13–15; *al-Tali'a al-Islamiyya*, August 1983, pp. 49–45. The main violent conflicts in the campus were between the Brothers and the PLO, as in the burning of the Red Cross offices headed by Haydar 'Abd al-Shafi in 1980 or the murder of Dr. Isma'il Khatib, member of *al-Mujamma'* by Fatah supporters in 1984. *Gaza Strip—Political Profile*, p. 41.

20. *Masirat al-Jihad al-Islami fi Filastin*, pp. 15–16; Shiqaqi, "Ma Hiyya Harakat al-Jihad al-Islami fi Filastin," in Sayyid Ahmad, Vol. 1, p. 348.

21. See, e.g., *al-Nur*, August 1980, pp. 13–15.

22. *Ha'aretz*, 15 March 1992; Shiqaqi, "Ma Hiyya Harakat al-Jihad al-Islami fi Filastin," pp. 348–49.

23. *Ha'aretz*, 20 January 1988; *al-Mujahid*, 28 June 1991.

24. *Masirat al-Jihad al-Islami fi Filastin*, p. 17; Israeli Civil Administration publication, *Informed Papers—the West Bank and the Gaza Strip*, Hebrew, November–December 1983, pp. 8–10.

25. Bashir Nafi', "Hawla Mafhum al-Nukhba wa-Mafhum al-Tali'a al-Risaliyya ," *al-Tali'a al-Islamiyya*, March, May, June 1983, pp. 36–37.

26. *Al-Nur*, 15 May 1982, pp. 33–41; Nafi', "al-Wahda min Khilal al-Ta'addud," ibid., pp. 61–62.

27. *Al-Tali'a al-Islamiyya*, May 1983, pp. 56–60.

28. Shiqaqi quoted in Sayyid Ahmad, Vol. 2, p. 730.

29. Sayyid Qutb, *Ma'alim fi al-Tariq* (Cairo, n.d.), pp. 7–8, 10–19; Shiqaqi. *al-Mashru' al-Islami al-Mu'asir wa-Markaziyyat al-Qadiyya al-Filastiniyya* (n.p., 1988), pp. 86–92; Nafi', "Tahawi al-'Askar wa Budhur al-Madd al-Islami," pp. 40–48.

30. *Al-'Alam* (London), 6 September 1986; *Masirat al-Jihad al-Islami fi Filastin*, p. 17; Shiqaqi's articles, "Janib al-Kaf am Janib al-Mikhraz," in Sayyid Ahmad, Vol. 1, pp. 626–627; "Ma Hiyya Harakat al-Jihad al-Islami fi Filastin," pp. 347–49.

31. 'Awda's interview in *al-Khalij*, 2 April 1989.

32. *Al-Tali'a al-Islamiyya*, May 1983, pp. 54–55; Shiqaqi's interview in *al-Liwa* (Amman), 3 October 1990.

33. Matti Steinberg, "The PLO and Palestinian Islamic Fundamentalism," *The Jerusalem Quarterly*, No. 52 (Fall 1989), pp. 45–46; Zamel, p. 198.

34. Muhsin Thabit, *Nashat al-Jama'a al-Islamiyya fi Sujun al-Ihtilal al-Israi'li* (n.p., n.d.), pp. 1–25. See also Paz, pp. 98–101.

35. Thabit, pp. 2–7, 21–24; *Koteret Rashit* (Tel Aviv), 21 October 1987, p. 9, 48.

36. *Al-Khalij*, 20 November 1987; *Ettela'at* (Tehran), 2 March 1993.

37. On Tamimi see *Harakat al-Jihad al-Islami Bayt al-Maqdis* (Amman, 1991), pp. 61–65.

38. On Fatah's attitude toward Islam see Steinberg, pp. 40–43.

39. *Al-Nur*, August 1980, p. 8.

40. Thabit, pp. 61–63; Ze'ev Schiff and Ehud Ya'ari, *Intifada* (New York, 1989), pp. 57–58.

41. *Al-'Alam*, 6 September 1986; Supreme Court decrees (Hebrew) 845/87, Vol. 42 (2), p. 55; Leaflets of the Islamic Jihad Squads were published also in *al-Tali'a al-Islamiyya*. See, e.g., November 1987, p. 57.

42. *Al-'Alam*, 6 September 1986; *al-Khalij*, 20 November 1987; Shiqaqi, "Ma Hiyya Harakat al-Jihad al-Islami fi Filastin," pp. 349–51.

43. Ahmad al-Qassem, "al-Jihad al-Islami 'ala Abwab al-Quds," *al-Mukhtar al-Islami*, March–April 1987, pp. 31–32.

44. *Al-Khalij*, 20 November 1987; *Masirat al-Jihad al-Islami fi Filastin*, pp. 20–21.

45. *Masirat al-Jihad al-Islami fi Filastin*, pp. 20–21.

46. *Al-Mujahid*, 4 October 1991.

47. Supreme Court decrees (Hebrew) 845/87, Vol. 42 (2), p. 54–55.

48. On 'Abdallah al-Shami see *al-Mujahid*, 16 March 1990.

49. 'Awda's interview in *al-Fajr* (Jerusalem), 22 November 1987.

50. *Kayhan al-'Arabi* (Tehran), 15 December 1988.

51. Jubran and Drake, p. 4.

52. Quoted in *Ha'aretz*, 16 February 1990.

53. Sami Zubaida, *Islam, the People and the State* (London, 1989), pp. 152–53.

54. Hala Mustafa, p. 82; Steinberg, p. 43; *Ha'aretz*, 30 June 1989.

55. Emmanuel Sivan, "Radical Islam—Comparative Aspects," in *Radical Islam: Hamas and the PLO at the Crossroad* (Hebrew; Jerusalem, February 1993), p. 9.

56. Leaflet dated from 11 December, appears in *Masirat al-Jihad al-Islami fi Filastin*, pp. 24–26.

57. On Hamas and its political platform see Hisham H. Ahmad, *Hamas from Religious Salvation to Political Transformation* (Jerusalem, 1994); Abu 'Amr, pp. 63–89.

58. Satloff, p. 393.

59. *Al-Qabas* (Kuwait), 4 February 1988.

60. "Al-Shuhada' al-Thalatha," in *al-Sabil fi Muraqabat al-Nafs wal-Tashih* (n.p., n.d.), pp. 43–47.

61. *Ha'aretz*, 12 April 1988; *al-Thawra al-Islamiyya* (London), May 1988.

62. On Islamic Jihad-Iran relations see chapter 5.

63. *Ha'aretz*, 8 April 1990; Paz, p. 66. On the Palestinian Islamic movements in Lebanon see *al-Majalla*, 27 September 1998.

64. Lababidi's interview in *Kayhan al-'Arabi*, 15 July 1989; Shaykh 'Abdallah al-Haliq's interview in *al-'Alam*, 3 February 1990; *al-Mujahid*, 12 July 1991.

65. On Islamic Jihad activity in the West see *Filastin wal-Intifada* (Chicago, April 1988); *al-Islam Tariq al-Intisar* (Chicago, June 1991). See also Shiqaqi's interview in *al-Liwa*, 3 October 1990; *Ha'aretz*, 5 June 1998; "The Islamic Jihad in South Florida: A Case Study," *Journal of Counterterrorism and Security International* (Spring 1998), pp. 58–62.

66. *Al-Sharq al-Awsat*, 17 December 1994; *Mideast Mirror*, 25 January 1995.

67. Boaz Ganor, "Islamic Jihad," *Matara*, No. 19 (1991), p. 30.

68. Shiqaqi's interviews in *al-Shihan* (Amman), 23 October 1993; *al-Majd* (Amman), 24 January 1995.

69. *Al-Mujahid*, 12 January 1990; Shiqaqi, "al-Ib'ad," in Sayyid Ahmad, Vol. 1, pp. 666–69.

70. *Al-Mujahid*, 12 July 1991.

71. See, e.g., *al-Mujahid*, 5, 29 January 1993; *al-Istiqlal* (Gaza), 12, 16 February 1996; *bi 'Inwan Ma'rakat al-Mujahid fi Aqbiyat al-Tahqiq* (n.p., n.d.), pp. 4–7, 20–22. The Islamic Jihad also operated at Internet Web site, titled The Voice of Jerusalem *(nida' al-Quds)*, which provided information about the movement and its ideological platform and surveyed events in Palestine. See <www.qudscall.com>

72. On Islamic Jihad's internal structure, see *al-Shira'* (Beirut), 4 January 1993; *al-La'iha al-Dakhiliyya* (hereafter, Islamic Jihad charter) (n.p., n.d.), especially pp. 13–33, 34–37,48–62; 'Azzam's interview in *al-Hayat al-Jadida* (Gaza), 16 January 1995; Shiqaqi's interview in *al-Sharq al-Awsat*, 17 March 1995.

73. *Al-Shira'*, 4 January 1993; Shiqaqi, "al-Mar'a al-Muslima," *al-Mukhtar al-Islami*, April 1980, pp. 64–70; *al-Nur*, August 1980, p. 19; *al-Mujahid*, December 1997. See also Islamic Jihad charter, pp. 10–11.

74. *Al-Shira'*, 4 January 1993; Shiqaqi, *al-Mashru' al-Islami al-Mu'asir wa-Markaziyyat al-Qadiyya al-Filastiniyya*, pp. 96–102; *Sawt al-Jama'a al-Islamiyya*, January 1993, p. 10.

75. See, e.g., *Harakat al-Jihad al-Islami Bayt al-Maqdis*, pp. 14–17; Ibrahim Sarbal, *Harakat al-Jihad al-Islami Kata'ib al-Aqsa* (Amman, 1990), pp. 58–67, 77–82.

Chapter Two

1. Shiqaqi and Nafi', "al-Qadiyya al-Filastiniyya," pp. 31–35.

2. Shiqaqi's interview in *al-Hayat*, 6 October 1994; Shalah's interview in *Majallat al-Dirasat al-Filastiniyya* (Beirut), 32 (Winter 1999), p. 99. See also *al-Tali'a al-Islamiyya*, May 1983, pp. 53–55.

3. 'Awda's interview in *al-Wahda al-Islamiyya* (Beirut), 29 April 1988; Shiqaqi's interview in *al-Khalij*, 27 August 1989; *al-Fajr*, 23 August 1988.

4. 'Awda's interview in *al-Islam wa-Filastin* (Nicosia), 5 October 1988. See also Nafi', "al-'Alam al-Islami wal-Qadiyya al-Filastiniyya," *al-Inasn*, December 1990, pp. 85–96.

5. Shiqaqi and Nafi', "al-Qadiyya al-Filastiniyya," pp. 31–35; Nafi''s articles, "Tahawi al-'Asakr wa-Budhur al-Madd al-Islami," pp. 40–48; "Asda' al-Suqut," *al-Mukhtar al-Islami*, April 1981, pp. 30–39.

6. Shiqaqi and Nafi', "al-Qadiyya al-Filastiniyya," pp. 31–35.

7. Tawfiq al-Tayyib, *al-Hall al-Islami ma ba'd al-Nakbatayn* (3rd edition, Cairo, 1985),

pp. 10–30.
8. 'Awda's interview in *al-Fajr*, 23 August 1987.
9. Shiqaqi, *al-Mashru' al-Islami al-Mu'asir wa-Markaziyyat al-Qadiyya al-Filastiniyya*, pp. 51–54, 70–80, 102–11.
10. Ibid., pp. 61–66, 68–81.
11. 'Awda's interview in *al-Fajr*, 23 August 1987; Shiqaqi and Nafi', "Masirat al-'Awda ila Allah," *al-Mukhtar al-Islami*, November 1980, pp. 23–35.
12. Shiqaqi, "Ma'alim fi al-Tariq," pp. 74–90; *al-Mujahid*, 15 January 1993.
13. Shiqaqi, *al-Mashru' al-Islami al-Mu'asir wa-Markaziyyat al-Qadiyya al-Filastiniyya*, pp. 86–92.
14. See, e.g., *Filastin Qadiyya Islamiyya* (n.p., n.d.); "Filastin fi Mashru' al-Nahda al-Islamiyya al-Mu'asira," *al-Islam wa-Filastin*, 31 January 1990, pp. 6–8.
15. Nafi', "al-Islam wal-Qadiyya al-Filastiniyya," *al-Tali'a al-Islamiyya*, January 1983, pp. 41–50; "Markaziyyat Qadiyyat al-Jihad," in *Filastin Qadiyya Islamiyya*, pp. 44–47; "Qadiyyat Filastin wa-Waqi' al-Umma al-Islamiyya," ibid., pp. 17–18; "al-Jihad fi Filastin," *al-Sabil*, 5 May 1989, p. 3.
16. "Markaziyyat Qadiyyat al-Jihad," p. 44–47; Shiqaqi, *al-Mashru' al-Islami al-Mu'asir wa-Markaziyyat al-Qadiyya al-Filastiniyya*, pp. 86–92.
17. Shiqaqi's interviews in *al-Wasat*, 30 January, *al-Sharq al-Awsat*, 17 March 1995.
18. "Al-Islamiyyun al-Filastiniyyun wal-Qadiyya al-Filastiniyya," *al-Islam wa-Filastin*, 3 March 1988, pp. 3–5.
19. On the concept of Jihad in the movement's outlook see "Qira'at fi Fiqh al-Shahada," *al-Islam wa-Filastin*, 5 June 1988, pp. 3–7. For a theological discussion of jihad in classical Islam, see Rudolph Peters, *Islam and Colonialism* (The Hague, 1979), pp. 9–37.
20. 'Awda, "al-Wala' wal-Bara' fi al-Qur'an," in *al-Islam Tariq al-Intisar*, pp. 30–33; 'Awda's interview in *al-Fajr*, 23 August 1987. See also Shiqaqi and Nafi' articles, "al-Nur wal-Dabab," *al-Mukhtar al-Islami*, March 1981, pp. 59–62; "al-Ta'rikh li-Madha," in Sayyid Ahmad, Vol. 1, pp. 318–30.
21. Shiqaqi, *al-Khumayni*, pp. 22–24, 32–38; "Fi Dhikra Murur 'Ammayn 'ala Intisar al-Thawra al-Islamiyya," *al-Mukhtar al-Islami*, March 1981, pp. 34–39; 'Awda, "Mawqif al-Islam min al-Istibdad al-Siyasi," *al-'Ahd* (Beirut), 25 March 1988, p. 7.
22. Shiqaqi, *al-Khumayni*, p. 33; "Iran al-Thawra wal-Dawla," in Sayyid Ahmad, Vol. 1, pp. 190–92.
23. Following the *hajj* accident 'Awda denounced the despotic rule of the Saudi family during preaching in al-Qassam mosque. Pictures of King Fahd were burned in front of the mosque. 'Awda, "Mawqif al-Islam min al-Istibdad al-Siyasi," p. 7. See also *al-Wahda al-Islamiyya*, March 1988.
24. Shiqaqi, *al-Khumayni*, pp. 40–42; 'Awda's interview in *al-Fajr*, 23 August 1987.
25. Shiqaqi, *al-Khumayni*, pp. 59–60; and his articles, "Fi Dhikra Murur 'Ammayn 'ala Intisar al-Thawra al-Islamiyya," pp. 40–42; "al-Sunna wal-Shi'a," in Sayyid

Ahmad, Vol. 1, pp. 273–96; "Arba'at A'wam 'ala Intisar al-Thawra al-Islamiyya," ibid., pp. 310–15.

26. Rekhess, p. 198.

27. Shiqaqi, "al-Sunna wal-Shi'a," pp. 281–82, 288–89.

28. See, e.g., Sivan, *Radical Islam*, p. 197; 'Abd al-Rahman Ibn Qasim, *Majmu' Fatawat Shaykh al-Islam Ahmad Ibn Taymiyya* (Cairo, n.p.), Vol. 3, pp. 278–79.

29. On Shaltut's biography see Kate Zebiri, *Mahmud Shaltut and Islamic Modernism* (Oxford, 1993).

30. Shiqaqi, *al-Khumayni*, pp. 48–49; and quoted in Sayyid Ahmad, Vol. 2, pp. 1304–307; Shiqaqi, "al-Sunna wal-Shi'a," pp. 274–76; 'Awda, "Mawqif al-Islam min al-Istibdad al-Siyasi," p. 7.

31. Shiqaqi's interview in *Kayhan al-'Arabi*, 29 December 1990; 'Awda's interview in *al-Fajr*, 23 August 1987.

32. Shiqaqi, *al-Khumayni*, pp. 47–48.

33. 'Abdallah al-Shami, "Kull al-Shu'ub Quddimat fa-Madha Qaddamna," *al-Istiqlal*, 31 July 1998, p. 14.

34. Shiqaqi, "al-Abad al-Haqiqiyya lil-Harb al-Iraniyya al-'Iraqiyya," *al-Mukhtar al-Islami*, December 1980, pp. 38–42; Shiqaqi quoted in Sayyid Ahmad, Vol. 2, pp. 558–64.

35. *Al-Mujahid*, 11 December 1992; 'Awda's interview in *al-Fikr al-Islami* (Beirut), June 1988, pp. 102–103; Sayyid Baraka's interview in *al-'Alam*, 13 January 1990.

36. 'Awda's interview in *al-Islam wa-Filastin*, 5 June 1988.

37. 'Awda's interview in *al-Khalij*, 2 April 1989; *al-Mujahid*, 2 February 1990.

38. 'Awda's interview in *al-'Ahd*, 22 April 1988.

39. Shiqaqi's interview in *al-Liwa*, 3 October 1990.

40. Shiqaqi's interview in *al-'Ahd*, 28 April 1989. This argument could be found also in *Masirat al-Jihad al-Islami fi Filastin*, pp. 26–27.

41. 'Awda's interview in *al-Khalij*, 2 April 1989; Shiqaqi's interview in *al-Wahda al-Islamiyya*, 9 September 1988; *al-Islam wa-Filastin*, 31 December 1989, pp. 12–13.

42. *Al-Islam wa-Filastin*, 31 December 1989, pp. 12–13.

43. Shiqaqi quoted in *al-'Alam*, 24 September 1988, pp. 16–17; Shiqaqi's interview in ibid., 13 October 1990. See also Ramadan Shalah, "al-Intifada fi 'Ammaha al-Thalith," in *al-Islam Tariq al-Intisar*, pp. 97–101.

44. *Al-Mujahid*, 1 February 1990.

45. Shiqaqi, "al-Intifada bayn al-Tafjir al-Islami wal-Istithmar al-'Almani," *al-'Alam*, 6 May 1989, pp. 32–33.

46. Ibid; *al-Islam wa-Filastin*, 28 June 1991, pp. 3–5.

47. Shiqaqi, *al-Istiqlal wal-Tab'iyya, al-Hawd al-'Arabi al-Islami* (n.p., n.d), pp. 3–5, 10–15.

48. Ibid., pp. 30–31; Shiqaqi, "Liqa' al-Tayyarat al-Islamiyya wal-Qawmiyya wal-Dimuqratiyya," in Sayyid Ahmad, Vol. 1, pp. 419–27. See also Shalah's interview in *al-Shira'*, 9 January 1996.

49. Shiqaqi quoted in Sayyid Ahmad, Vol. 1, p. 676; and his articles, "Liqa' al-Tayyarat al-Islamiyya wal-Qawmiyya wal-Dimuqratiyya," p. 426; "al-Usuliyya wal-'Almaniyya," *al-Hayat*, 28 July 1995; Shalah's interview in *al-Shira'*, 29 January 1996; and quoted in *al-Istiqlal*, 4 September 1998, p. 15.
50. Shiqaqi, "Ma'alim fi al-Tariq," p. 90.
51. Shiqaqi, "Liqa' al-Tayyarat al-Islamiyya wal-Qawmiyya wal-Dimuqratiyya," p. 427; Shiqaqi's interviews in *al-Khalij*, 27 August 1989; *al-'Aqida* (Algiers), 17 October 1990; *al-Majd* (Amman), 24 October 1994.
52. Islamic Jihad charter, p. 4. See also Shiqaqi's interview in *al-Hayat*, 6 October 1994; *al-Tali'a al-Islamiyya*, March 1983, pp. 32–37.
53. Sayyid Ahmad, Vol. 1, p. 89.

Chapter Three

1. Steinberg, p. 42.
2. Ibid., p. 30.
3. 'Awda's interview in *al-Fajr*, 23 August 1987. See also *al-Tali'a al-Islamiyya*, August 1983, pp. 50–56.
4. "Al-Ma'sat al-Filastiniyya Akhir al-Lil," *al-Tali'a al-Islamiyya*, August 1983, pp. 41–42. See also Abu 'Amr, p. 109.
5. "Al-Ma'sat al-Filastiniyya Akhir al-Lil," pp. 24–25, 35–36.
6. Ibid., pp. 35–41.
7. Shiqaqi, "Risala ila Yasir 'Arafat," in Sayyid Ahmad, Vol. 1, 630–31.
8. See, e.g., Haydar 'Abd al-Shafi's interview in *al-Majalla* (London), 25 November 1987; Rashid al-Shawwa quoted in Jerusalem Domestic Service, 10 December—DR, 11 December 1987.
9. 'Arafat's interviews in *al-Yawm al-Sabi'* (Paris), 23 November 1987, *Filastin al-Thawra* (Nicosia), 21 January 1988.
10. Salim al-Za'anun's interview in *al-Majalla*, 25 November 1987; Sa'ih's interview in *al-Akhbar* (Cairo), 15 December 1987. The Islamic Jihad denied any affiliation with Hourani, accusing 'Arafat of an attempt to introduce the movement as part of the PLO. Hourani's interview in *al-Siyasa* (Kuwait), 24 January 1990; *al-Mujahid*, 2 February 1990.
11. Abu Iyyad's interview in *al-Mujtama'* (Kuwait), 17 November 1987.
12. Ibid.
13. Za'anun's interview in *al-Majalla*, 25 November 1987.
14. Abu Jihad's interview in *al-Yawm al-Sabi'*, 1 February 1988.
15. On the 19th PNC conference see Joshua Teitelbaum, "The Palestinian Liberation Organization," *MECS*, Vol. XII (1988), pp. 246–54.
16. On Iran-PLO relations after the Islamic Revolution see David Menashri, *Iran: A Decade of War* (New York, 1990), pp. 253–54.

17. *Al-Islam wa-Filastin*, 30 December 1988, p. 15.
18. Ibid; Shiqaqi, "al-Taharruk wal-Fikr al-Filastini amam Masar al-Taswiya," in Sayyid Ahmad, Vol. 1, pp. 392–401.
19. 'Awda's interview in *al-Khalij*, 2 April 1989; Shiqaqi's interview in ibid., 27 August 1989; "al-Islam Khatt al-Difa' al-Awwal 'an Filastin," in *Filsatin Qadiyya Islamiyya*, p. 31.
20. *Al-Mujahid*, 27 April 1989, 3 May 1991.
21. Shiqaqi's interview in *Kayhan al-'Arabi*, 21 August 1993.
22. 'Awda quoted in *al-Mujahid*, 27 April 1990.
23. *Al-Mujahid*, 22 September, 27 October 1989, 16 February 1990.
24. Shiqaqi's interviews in *al-Liwa*, 3 October 1990; *al-Ribat* (Athens), 14 May 1991. See also Shami's interview in *al-Hayat al-Jadida* (Gaza), 2 January 1995.
25. Shiqaqi's interview in *al-Liwa*, 3 October 1990.
26. *Al-Mujahid*,13, 27 April 1990; *al Ribat*, 12 May 1992.
27. 'Abdallah 'Isa, *Hafilat al-Jihad al-Islami* (Amman, 1991), pp. 9–18, 45–50.
28. 'Isa, pp. 65–72; *Harakat al-Jihad al-Islami Bayt al-Maqdis*, pp. 1–15, 30–33, 51–52; *al-Islam wa-Filastin*, 20 June 1990; Tamimi's interview in *al-Usbu' al-'Arabi*, 4 October 1993; *al-Bilad*, 23 November 1994.
29. *Al-Islam wa-Filastin*, 20 June 1990; al-Ribat, 19 May 1992.
30. *Al-Mujahid*, April 1991, 27 September 1991; Shiqaqi's interview in *al-'Ahd*, 28 April 1988.
31. Shiqaqi quoted in Sayyid Ahmad, Vol. 2, p. 806.
32. *Al-Mujahid*, 3 May, 20 September 1991.
33. Ibid., 20 May 1991.
34. Quoted in Helena Cobban, "The PLO and the Intifada," *MEJ*, Vol. 44 (Spring 1990), pp. 214–15.
35. *Al-Islam wa-Filastin*, 1 April 1988, pp. 3–4; *al-Thawra al-Islamiyya*, November 1990. For a similar distinction about the PLO in Hamas's attitude see *Filastin al-Muslima*, May 1990.
36. *Filastin al-Thawra*, 8 July 1990, pp. 1–8. The article was written in response to a booklet distributed by Hamas in the territories under the title *Hamas bayn Alam al-Waqi' wa-Amal al-Mustaqbal* ("Hamas between the Reality of Distress and Hopes for the Future"), in which it posited itself as a political alternative to the PLO.
37. *Al-Mujahid*, 21 December 1990.
38. Shiqaqi's interview in *al-'Ahd*, 28 April 1989. *Al-Islam wa-Filastin*, 28 June 1991, pp. 3–5.
39. See, e.g., *al-Islam wa-Filastin*, 15 October 1989; *al-Mujahid*, 9 August, 6 September 1991.
40. On the Palestinian left and the religious revival in the territories see Steinberg, pp. 46–49.
41. Habash's interview in *al-Hadaf* (Damascus), December 1987; *Tariq al-Intisar* (Nicosia), 1 November 1987, pp. 26–27.

42. Habash's interview in *al-Hadaf*, December 1987; *al-Hurriya* (Nicosia), 18 September 1988, pp. 6–9.
43. *Tariq al-Intisar*, 4 May 1988, pp. 26–27.
44. Ibid; Habash's interview in *al-Hadaf*, December 1987.
45. *Al-Safir* (Beirut), 30 March 1989, p. 9; *al-Islam wa-Filastin*, 20 April 1990, p. 2.
46. Shiqaqi's interviews in *al-'Ahd*, 28 April 1989; *al-Khalij*, 27 August 1989.
47. *Al-Mujahid*, 28 September 1990.
48. *Al-Islam wa-Filastin*, 20 April 1990. See also *Filastin al-Muslima*, April 1990, p. 8.
49. On Iran-PFLP-GC relations see *Ha'aretz*, 19 December 1989.
50. *Hiwar ma' Ahmad Jibril: al-Thawra wal-Mutaghayyirat al-Dawliyya* (Damascus, 1990), pp. 39–42.
51. Muhammad Zakariyya, "al-Intifada wal-Islah al-Tanzimi fi Munazzamat al-Tahrir al-Filastini," *al-Fikr al-Dimuqrati*, Vol. 5 (Winter 1988), pp. 22–31.
52. *Al-Mujahid*, 13 September 1991.
53. Ibid., 1 November 1991.
54. Shiqaqi's interview in *al-'Ahd*, 24 April 1989; Habash's interview in *Filastin al-Muslima*, December 1991; Jibril's interview in *al-'Alam*, 28 April 1990.
55. Sayyid Baraka's interview in *al-'Alam*, 13 January 1990.
56. Shiqaqi's interview in *al-Khalij*, 27 August 1989; 'Awda's interview in *al-Fajr*, 23 August 1987; Shiqaqi and Nafi',"al-Qadiyya al-Filastiniyya," pp. 30–32.
57. 'Awda's interview in *al-Fajr*, 23 August 1987; Shiqaqi's interview in *al-Liwa*, 3 October 1990; *al-Mujahid*, 3 November 1989. See also "Fi al-'Alaqa bayn al-Da'iya wal-Mad'u," *Fi Sabil Jabha Islamiyya Mutahidah* (n.p., n.d.), pp. 41–43.
58. *Al-Wahda al-Islamiyya*, 29 April 1988.
59. Shiqaqi, *al-Mashru' al-Islami al-Mu'asir wa-Markaziyyat al-Qadiyya al-Filastiniyya*, pp. 86–92; Shiqaqi's interview in *al-Liwa*, 3 October 1990; *al-Tali'a al-Islamiyya*, May 1983, pp. 52–53; 'Awda's interview in *al-Fajr*, 23 August 1987.
60. *Al-Fajr*, 23 August 1987. See also Islamic Jihad charter, pp. 4, 8.
61. *Islamic Activity in the West Bank*, p. 24; On the Brothers' communal activity prior to the Intifada see bin Yusuf, pp. 55–90; Milton-Edwards, pp. 104–55.
62. *Islamic Activity in the West Bank*, p. 24.
63. 'Anabtawi quoted in ibid., p. 25. A more moderate stance was adopted by Shaykh Bassam Jarar, ibid., pp. 24–25.
64. Abu 'Amr, pp. 157–58.
65. Steinberg, p. 53.
66. On the friction within the Brothers, see al-Jarbawi, pp. 108–11. For literature on Hamas see Ahmad, *Hamas from Religious Salvation to Political Transformation*; Abu 'Amr, pp. 63–89; Meir Litvak, "The Islamization of the Palestinian-Israeli Conflict: The Case of Hamas," *MES*, Vol. 34, No. 1 (January 1998), pp. 148–63; Shaul Mishal and Avraham Sela, *The Palestinian Hamas: Visions, Violence, and Coexistence* (New York, 1999).
67. *Davar* (Tel-Aviv), 5 May 1989, p. 22.

68. *Filastin al-Muslima*, April 1990, p. 25.
69. *Mithaq Harakat al-Muqawama al-Islamiyya—Filastin (Hamas)* (n.p., 1988), clause 2.
70. *Al-'Alam*, 2 September 1988; Husam al-Nasir, *Hamas al-Intilaq wa-Mu'adalat al-Sira'* (n.p, n.d.), pp. 2–6.
71. See also Thabit, pp. 27–61.
72. *Al-Mujahid*, 18 May, 28 December 1990, 24 April 1992.
73. Shiqaqi's interviews in *al-Wahda al-Islamiyya*, 9 September 1988; *al-'Alam*, 1 October 1990; *al-Mujahid*, 21, 28 December 1990, 24 April 1992.
74. 'Awda's interview in *al-'Alam*, 27 January 1990.
75. *Al-Islam wa-Filastin*, 3 March 1988, p. 3; ibid., 1 August 1988, pp. 3–4.
76. *Al-Thawra al-Islamiyya*, 10 November 1988, p. 40.
77. *Al-Mujahid*, 14, 28 September 1990; Shiqaqi quoted in *al-Liwa*, 10 July 1992.
78. *Filastin al-Muslima*, April 1990, p. 25.
79. 'Imad al-'Alami's interview in *Filastin al-Muslima*, December 1990.
80. *Ha'aretz*, 12 January 1990; *Filastin al-Muslima*, April 1990, p. 25.
81. *Sawt al-Aqsa* (Bonn), 15 January 1990, p. 1; *Filastin al-Muslima*, April 1990, p. 25.
82. *Mithaq*, clauses 6, 27; bin Yusuf, pp. 144–47.
83. *The Jerusalem Report*, 29 November 1990, p. 39.
84. See, e.g., *al-Sha'b* (Cairo), 5 December 1989; *al-Mujahid*, 8 June 1990, 27 July 1991; *al-Umma* (San'a'), November 1991; *Filastin al-Muslima*, June 1992.
85. Tehran International Service in Arabic, 11 June—DR, 12 June 1990; *Filastin al-Muslima*, March 1991.
86. *Filastin al-Muslima*, March 1991, p. 41.
87. On the Gulf states' support of Hamas, see *al-Ahdath* (Beirut), 20 August 1990.
88. On Palestinian Islam and the Gulf crises see Iyyad al-Barghuthi, *al-Haraka al-Islamiyya al-Filastiniyya wal-Nizam al-'Alami al-Jadid* (Jerusalem, 1992), pp. 69–72, 81–86. See also Shiqaqi's interview in *al-Masa'* (Beirut), 26 December 1991; *al-Mujahid*, 10 August 1990.
89. *Al-Umma* (Beirut), February 1992, p. 6.
90. *Al-Hurriya*, 27 September 1992, p. 14–15.
91. See, e.g., Khalid al-Harub, "Harakat Hamas wal-Ta'ddudidyya al-Diniyya wal-Siyasiyya," in Jawad Ahmad and Iyyad al-Barghuthi (eds.), *Dirasa fi al-Fikr al-Siyasi li-Hamas* (Amman, 1997), pp. 181–83.
92. Habash's interview in *Filastin al-Muslima*, December 1991, p. 19. On the Islamic Jihad's disappointment at the weak functioning of the Palestinian opposition see *al-Mujahid*, 4 December 1992.

Chapter Four

1. *Al-Mujahid*, 22 January 1993.
2. 'Arafat's interview in *Akhir Sa'a* (Cairo), January 1993; *al-Mujahid*, 22, 29 January,

23 April 1993.

3. Shiqaqi's interviews in *al-Kifah*, 18 October; *al-Mujahid*, 29 October 1993; *al-Quds*, 10 January 1994.

4. *Al-Sabil*, October 1993, p. 1. See also Shiqaqi, "Didda al-Sharq al-Awsat al-Jadid," in Sayyid Ahmad, Vol. 1, pp. 569–72.

5. Islamic Jihad charter, p. 12.

6. Shiqaqi quoted in *al-Risala* (Gaza), 20 May 1994; ibid., 21 August 1994.

7. Shiqaqi's interviews in *al-Risala*, 21 August 1994; *al-Quds*, 15 May, 19 July 1994.

8. *Al-Mujahid*, 5 January 1993.

9. On suicide attacks in the Lebanon context see Martin Kramer, "Sacrifice and Self-Martyrdom in Shi'ite Lebanon," idem. *Arab Awakening and Islamic Revival* (New Brunswick, 1996), pp. 231–41. See also Haggay Ram, *Myth and Mobilization in Revolutionary Iran* (Washington, D.C., 1994), pp. 69–87.

10. Shiqaqi's interview in *al-Sharq al-Awsat*, 17 March

11. See, e.g., Shiqaqi's interviews in *al-Majd*, 24 January 1995; *al-Khalij*, 25 January 1995; and in Sayyid Ahmad, Vol. 2, p. 1103.

12. *Ma'ariv*, 12 April 1994; *al-Hayat*, 5 June 1994; *al-Istiqlal*, 18 November 1994.

13. *Al-Mujahid*, 15 January 1994. See also Anders Strindberg, "The Damascus-Based Alliance of Palestinian Forces: A Primer," *Journal of Palestinian Studies*, Vol. 24, No. 3 (Spring 2000), pp. 60–76.

14. *Al-Hayat*, 25 July 1994.

15. Ibid., 24 April 1994; Ibrahim Ghawsha's interview in *al-Sabil*, 31 May 1994; Zahhar's interview in *al-Hayat al-Jadida*, 2 January 1995.

16. Hawatmeh quoted in *Mideast Mirror*, 25 January

17. Shiqaqi, "Azmat al-Mu'arada al-Filastiniyya," in Sayyid Ahmad, Vol. 1, pp. 679–83; Shiqaqi's interviews in *al-Mujahid*, 29 October 1993; *al-Wasat*, 1 December 1994.

18. Shiqaqi, "Azmat al-Mu'arida al-Filastiniyya," p. 683.

19. *Al-Mujahid*, 13 January 1994; Shiqaqi's interviews in *al-Quds*, 20 April 1994; *al-Hayat*, 6 October 1994.

20. Zahhar's interview in *al-Hayat al-Jadida*, 2 January 1995; 'Azzam quoted in ibid., 9 January 1995.

21. See, e.g., *al-Safir*, 25 August 1994; *Filastin al-Muslima*, May 1995; *al-Hayat*, 26 September 1996.

22. Shiqaqi's interview in *al-Masa'* (Beirut), 26 December 1991; *al-Mujahid*, 15 January 1993; al-Quds, 2 April 1994; *al-Istiqlal*, 30 December 1994, 13 January 1995.

23. *Al-Mujahid*, 15 April 1994; *al-Risala*, 21 August 1994; *Sawt al-Jama'a al-Islamiyya*, December 1992.

24. Shiqaqi's interview in *al-Masa'*, 26 December 1991; 'Azzam's interview in *al-Hayat al-Jadida*, 16 January 1995.

25. The Islamic Jihad depicted Tamimi's withdrawal from the PLO and his refusal to rejoin any PA bodies as a welcome step, but also as coming "too late." In fact, the

rivalry between the two factions remained, and was even heightened by Tamimi's dissociation from Iran, which he blamed for failing to disseminate its revolutionary message due to its narrow Shi'ite perspective. Additionally, Tamimi refused to join the forum of the Ten Palestinian Factions because of his aversion to the Marxist ideology of its leftist member groups, whom, he insisted, must adopt Islam as a condition for his cooperation. The Islamic Jihad-Jerusalem, however, found itself in an inferior position. The breach with the PLO left the movement with no political or financial resources. Tamimi's death in 1998 ultimately left his faction without any significant leadership. See Tamimi's interviews in *al-Hawadith*, 26 August 1994; *al-Watan al-'Arabi*, 2 December 1988; and *al-Hadith* (Amman), 28 October 1996. On his death see *al-Quds al-'Arabi*, 23 March 1998.

26. *Al-Quds*, 12, 18 September 1993; *al-Nahar* (Beirut), 27 May 1994. See also 'Ali al-Jarbawi, "Mawqif al-Harakat al-Islamiyya min al-Ittifaq al-Filastini al-Isra'ili," *al-Mustaqbal al-'Arabi*, February 1994, pp. 57–58.

27. Shiqaqi's interview in *al-'Alam*, June 1994; *al-Mujtama'*, 29 November 1994; *al-Wasat*, 30 January 1995.

28. See, e.g., *al-Istiqlal*, 21 October 1994.

29. Ibid.

30. On the civil society concept see Augustus R. Norton, "Introduction," in idem. *Civil Society in the Middle East* (Leiden, 1995), Vol. 1, pp. 11–12; Ernest Gellner, *Conditions of Liberty: Civil Society and its Rivals* (New York, 1994).

31. On civil society in the Arab world see Norton, pp. 6–18; Meir Litvak (ed.), *Islam and Democracy in the Arab World* (Hebrew; Tel Aviv, 1998).

32. On PA-civil society in the territories see Muhammad Muslih, "Palestinian Civil Society," in Norton (ed.), *Civil Society in the Arab World*, Vol. 1, pp. 243–68; Sara Roy, "Civil Society in the Gaza Strip: Obstacles to Social Reconstruction," ibid., Vol. 2, pp. 221–58.

33. Elie Rekhess and Meir Litvak, "Palestinian Affairs," *MECS*, Vol. XIX (1995), pp. 146–47.

34. Tayyib 'Abd al-Rahim quoted in *al-Hayat al-Jadida*, 7 January 1998.

35. Sayyid Ahmad, p. 111; Shiqaqi quoted in *al-Hayat*, 28 July 1995.

36. Shiqaqi quoted in *al-Hayat*, 28 July 1995.

37. Shiqaqi's interview in *al-Hayat*, 6 October 1994; Shiqaqi, "al-Mar'a al-Muslima," pp. 64–70; *al-Nur*, August 1980, pp. 13–15.

38. Shiqaqi's articles, "Ma'rakat al-Mushaf wal-'Askar," in Sayyid Ahmad, Vol. 2, pp. 1597–99; "Irhab al-Muthaqqafin didda al-Islamiyyin," ibid., Vol. 1, pp. 402–18; and Shiqaqi quoted in *al-Hayat*, 28 July 1995.

39. Shiqaqi quoted in Sayyid Ahmad, Vol. 2, pp. 728, 1219–20; and in *al-Majd*, 24 October 1994.

40. Shiqaqi quoted in Sayyid Ahmad, Vol. 2, p. 728. See also *al-Tali'a al-Islamiyya*, May 1983, pp. 50–53.

41. On the *shura* and its modern meanings see Ami Ayalon, *Language and Change in*

the Arab Middle East (New York, 1987), pp. 119–23.

42. Shiqaqi quoted in Sayyid Ahmad, Vol. 2, pp. 726–27; al-Mujahid, 3 November 1989. See also Islamic Jihad charter, pp. 7–8.

43. Shiqaqi quoted in Sayyid Ahmad, Vol. 2, pp. 725–26; al-Hayat, 6 October 1994, 28 July 1995.

44. Nafi', "Hawla Mafhum al-Nakhba," p. 37; Muhammad al-Hindi quoted in al-Risala, 24 September 1998.

45. Shiqaqi's interview in Kayhan al-'Arabi, 25 January 1994.

46. Jamil Hamami quoted in al-Siyasa al-Filastiniyya (Summer–Winter 1997), pp. 133–42. See also Harub, pp. 175–78.

47. Al-Risala, 24 September 1998; Shalah quoted in al-Istiqlal, 4 September 1998. See also Hamas publication, al-Dimuqratiyya Da'ia (Gaza, 1994).

48. Afkar Siyasiyya li-Hizb al-Tahrir, pp. 135–40.

49. Shiqaqi's interview in al-Mujtama', 29 November 1994; 'Azzam's interview in al-Hayat al-Jadida, 16 January 1995. For Hamas-PA relations see Menachem Klein, "Competing Brothers: The Web of Hamas-PLO Relations," in Bruce Maddy-Weitzman and Efraim Inbar (eds.), Religious Radicalism in the Greater Middle East (London, 1997), pp. 123–24, 128.

50. Shami's interview in al-Hayat al-Jadida, 2 January 1995; al-Mujahid, 15 May 1995; Shiqaqi's interview in al-Majd, 22 May 1995; 'Azzam's interview in al-Hayat al-Jadida, 16 January 1995.

51. See, e.g., Meir Hatina, "Hamas and the Oslo Accords: Religious Dogma in a Changing Political Reality," Mediterranean Politics, Vol. 4, No. 3 (Autumn 1999), pp. 46–50.

52. Abu Samara's faction unilaterally accrued the entire record of the Islamic Jihad to itself, using both the movement's name as well as that of its organ, al-Mujahid. On the Jihad factions that participated in the PA bodies see al-Quds, 7 January 1995; al-Mujahid (Gaza), 24 April, 13 June, 1 August 1997; al-Majalla, 27 September 1998; al-Bashir (Gaza), December 1998, January 1999. The Islamic Jihad, for its part, continued to display contempt for all rival factions, whom it viewed as nothing more than titles with no ideological of organizational justification. See al-Istiqlal, 2 October 1998.

53. Al-Mujahid (Gaza), 13 June 1997.

54. Klein, pp. 123–24.

55. Shami's interview in al-Quds, 7 May 1994; al-Wasat, 19 September 1994; Shiqaqi's interview in al-Majd, 21 November 1994; and quoted in Sayyid Ahmad, Vol. 2, pp. 1357–61. See also Filastin al-Muslima, December 1993.

56. Nasir Yusuf's interview in Filastin al-Muslima, December 1994; Diyab al-Luh quoted in al-Karama, 7 September 1995.

57. On the 1996 elections in the territories see Elie Rekhess and Meir Litvak, "Palestinian Affairs," MECS, Vol. XX (1996), pp. 138–48.

58. Al-Istiqlal, 26 January, 16 February 1996; Shami's interview in al-Hayat al-Jadida, 2

January 1995.

59. *Filastin al-Muslima*, January 1994; *al-Sabil*, 7 January 1997. See also Bernd Schoch, *The Islamic Movement: A Challenge for Palestinian State-Building* (Jerusalem, 1999), pp. 89–92.

60. See, e.g., *al-Mujahid*, 5 January 1996; *al-Istiqlal*, 12 January 1996.

61. See *Ha'aretz*, 25 May 1995, 14 October 1996; *al-Hayat*, 31 May, 1 June 1195; *al-Istiqlal*, 19 May 1995; Baraka's interview in *al-Watan al-'Arabi*, 24 October 1997.

62. 'Awda quoted in *al-Mujahid*, 12 March 1993.

63. Upon his withdrawal from the Islamic Jihad, Baraka was involved in the establishment of Palestinian Hizballah, together with Ahmad Muhanna, and later in the convening of a body called the "Council of Palestinian 'Ulama'." This forum focused its activity on the Palestinian refugee camps in Lebanon. Baraka's interview in *al-Watan al-'Arabi*, 24 October 1997; *al-Majalla*, 27 September 1998.

64. Shiqaqi's interviews in *al-Majd*, 24 October 1994; *al-Hayat*, 31 May 1995; *al-Liwa*, 14 June 1995.

65. S.N. Eisenstadt (ed.), *Max Weber on Charisma and Institution Building* (Chicago, 1968), pp. 48–60.

66. *Fathi al-Shiqaqi Shahidan* (Beirut, 1996), pp. 17–18; Sayyid Ahmad, Vol. 2, pp. 1618–24.

67. *Fathi al-Shiqaqi Shahidan*, pp. 19–20; *Ha'aretz*, 3 November 1995.

68. *Ma'ariv*, 31 October, 2 November 1995. On the reactions in the Arab world to Shiqaqi's death see *Fathi al-Shiqaqi Shahidan*.

69. On Shalah biography see *al-Bilad*, 13 January 1996; Shalah's interview in *al-Bayadir al-Siyasi*, 14 September 1996.

70. *Al-Watan al-'Arabi*, 8 March 1996; Baraka's interview in ibid., 24 October 1997. PA representatives made an effort to approach these veterans of the Islamic Jihad, such as Baraka and 'Awda, who, frustrated by Shiqaqi's centralist conduct, dissociated themselves from the movement in the early 1990s. Eventually, Baraka and 'Awda returned to the Gaza Strip with the blessing of the PA and the consent of Israel (April 1999, March 2000). Baraka was appointed vice secretary general in the Youth and Sport Ministry of the PA in Gaza. As for 'Awda, he was allowed to return to his pre-Intifada post as preacher in the al-Qassam mosque in Bayt Lahiyya. This episode was of little significance to the Islamic Jihad's status, since the two men had suspended their activity in the movement long before the Oslo Accords and the establishment of the PA. Moreover, contrary to 'Arafat's expectations, they argued that they represented only themselves. See *al-Hayat*, 30 April 1999; *al-Majd*, 7 June 1999; *al-Majalla* 13 March 2000.

71. Shalah quoted in *Fathi al-Shiqaqi Shahidan*, pp. 30–34, and also in Sayyid Ahmad, Vol. 1, pp. 15–19; *al-Istiqlal*, 1 December 1995; *al-Bilad*, 13 January 1996.

72. Shalah's interview in *al-Shira'*, 29 January 1996; *Majallat al-Dirasat al-Filastiniyya* (Winter 1999), pp. 98–99. See also Shami's interview in *al-Hayat al-Jadida*, 2 January 1995.

73. Shalah's interviews in *al-Bilad*, 13 January; *al-'Ahd*, 2 February 1996; and *al-Istiqlal*, 9 February 1996.
74. On the February–March attacks and the PA reaction see Rekhess and Litvak, "Palestinian Affairs," *MECS*, Vol. XX (1996), pp. 158–60.
75. Shalah's interview in *al-Shira'*, 29 January 1996.
76. See, e.g., *al-Quds*, 26 May 1996; *al-Ra'y* (Amman), 26 May, 15 August 1996; *Filastin al-Muslima*, July 1996.
77. *Al-Istiqlal*, 16 February 1996, 16 October 1998; 'Azzam quoted in ibid., 16 October 1998.
78. Yasin's interview in *al-Istiqlal*, 17 July 1998; Muhammad Nazzal's interview in *al-Watan al-'Arabi*, 17 November 1997; *al-Ayyam* (Ramallah, West Bank), 3 November 1997.

Chapter Five

1. On Sunni radicals' attitude toward the Islamic Revolution see Sivan, pp. 181–99.
2. Martin Kramer, "Concluding Chapter: The Shi'a Renewal," in idem. *Protest and Revolution in Shi'a Islam* (Hebrew; Tel Aviv, 1985), p. 154.
3. See, e.g., Sa'id Hawwa, *al-Khumayniyya Shudhudh fi al-'Aqa'id wa Shudhudh fi al-Mawaqif* (Cairo, 1987).
4. Hawwa, pp. 3–4.
5. 'Awda's interview in *al-Thawra al-Islamiyya*, May 1988; Shiqaqi's interview in *al-'Ahd*, 28 April 1989.
6. Shiqaqi quoted in *al-'Ahd*, 2 September 1988.
7. *Al-Thawra al-Islamiyya*, February 1988.
8. Shaykh Hasan al-Safar quoted in *al-Thawra al-Islamiyya*, February 1988; *Kayhan International* (Tehran), 2 July 1990.
9. Tehran Press agency, 11 January 1988, as quoted by the BBC.
10. *Foreign Report*, 11 May 1988; *al-Dustur* (Beirut), 30 October, 20 November 1989; *al-Usbu' al-'Arabi* (Beirut), 9 October 1989.
11. *Al-'Alam*, 7 January 1989; *al-Mujahid*, 25 October 1991; *al-Hilal al-Duwali* (Tehran), 16 November 1991.
12. See, e.g., Muhammad Nazzal's interview in *al-Watan al-'Arabi*, 30 October 1992; *al-Muharir* (Paris), 23 November 1992.
13. *Al-Hilal al-Duwali*, 16 November 1991.
14. On Hizballah's ideological affinity to Iran see Martin Kramer, "Redeeming Jerusalem: The Pan-Islamic Premise of Hizballah," in David Menashri (ed.), *The Iranian Revolution and the Muslim World*, pp. 106–26.
15. Fadlallah quoted in *Filastin al-Muslima*, November 1991.
16. Fadlallah quoted in *al-'Alam*, 13 November, pp. 32–33; Fadlallah, "Ab'ad Ittifaq Ghazza-Ariha fi al-Waqi' al-Filastini wal-'Arabi," *Qira'at Siyasiyya*, Vol. 4 (Win-

ter 1994), pp. 85–94.

17. *Al-Khabr* (Algiers), 25 September 1991; *al-Mujahid*, 5 July 1991.

18. *Al-Mujahid*, 5 July 1991. See also Shiqaqi's interview in *al-Wasat*, 30 January 1995.

19. Shiqaqi quoted in *al-Mujahid*, 21 February 1992. See also Sayyid Ahmad, Vol. 2, pp. 1349–52.

20. *Al-Mujahid*, 21 February 1992.

21. *Al-Quds al-'Arabi*, 2 April 1992; *al-Mujahid*, December 1997.

22. *Al-'Ahd*, 6 May 1994; *Filastin al-Muslima*, May 1995.

23. See, e.g., Shiqaqi's interview in *al-Sharq al-Awsat*, 1 January 1995; and quoted in Sayyid Ahmad, Vol. 2, pp. 1305–307.

24. Shiqaqi's interviews in *al-Wasat*, 19 September 1994, 30 January 1995; *al-Sharq al-Awsat*, 17 March 1995. See also Shami and 'Azzam's interviews in *al-Hayat al-Jadida*, 2, 16 January 1995.

25. Shiqaqi's interview in *al-Liwa*, 3 October; also Shami and 'Azzam's interviews in *al-Hayat al-Jadida*, 2, 16 January 1995.

26. As discussed above (Chapter Three) Tamimi and his faction abandoned their ecumenical attitude after what they perceived as Iran's failure in promoting pan-Islamic unity. See also note 25 to Chapter Four.

27. *Sawt al-Jama'a al-Islamiyya*, December 1992; Shalah quoted in *al-Istiqlal*, 28 August 1998; ibid., 21 August, 25 September 1998.

28. On revolution and pragmatism in Iranian policy see Menashri, pp. 386–93.

29. See, e.g., *al-Watan al-'Arabi*, 18 December 1992.

30. On Khatami's Iran and the Arab world see David Menashri, "Iran," *MECS*, Vol. XXI (1997), pp. 350–58; Meir Hatina, "Egypt", ibid., pp. 334–35.

31. *Al-Sha'b*, *al-'Ahd*, 3 November 1995; Nasarallah quoted in *Fathi al-Shiqaqi Shahidan*, p. 35. See also Khamene'i and Fadlallah quoted in *al-Mujahid*, 2 October 1997.

32. Khalil al-Quqa's interview in *al-Anba'* (Kuwait), 8 October 1988.

33. Quqa's interview in *al-'Alam*, 26 January 1991.

34. On Hamas-Iran relations see Hatina, "Iran and the Palestinian Islamic Movement," pp. 113–19.

35. See, e.g., Nazzal's interview in *al-Diyar* (Beirut), 25 October 1994; Ghawsha's interview in *al-Shuruq* (Sharja, UAE), 22 April 1996; Tehran Voice of the Islamic Republic of Iran, 9 March—DR, 11 March 1996.

Chapter Six

1. Emmanuel Sivan, *Arab Political Myths* (Hebrew; Tel Aviv, 1988), pp. 168–69.

2. See, e.g., Ernest Cassirer, *Language and Myth* (New York, 1946), pp. 1–17; Ofra Bengio, *Saddam's Word: Political Discourse in Iraq* (Oxford, 1998), pp. 4–6.

3. *Al-Mujahid*, 26 February, 23 April 1993. On the jihad doctrine in Islam see Majid Khadduri, *War and Peace in the Law of Islam* (Baltimore, 1955), pp. 55–73.

4. "Ma' al-Aswa' al-Husna fi al-Hurub," in *Filastin Qadiyya Islamiyya*, pp. 63–64; 'Awda quoted in *al-Mujahid*, 24 April 1991.

5. "Qira'at fi Fiqh al-Shahada," p. 12. According to Zamel, the author was Misbah al-Suri, who was killed in the Shaja'iyya event in October 1987; Zamel, p. 195.

6. *Al-Mujahid*, 30 October 1992, 3 December 1993; *al-Istiqlal*, 26 January 1996, 21 August 1998; Shiqaqi quoted in Sayyid Ahmad, Vol. 2, p. 1137.

7. *Al-Mujahid*, 2 August 1991.

8. Ibid., 26 July 1991.

9. On the difference between martyrdom and immolation see "Qira'at fi Fiqh al-Shahada," p. 3–4. See also Franz Rosental, "Intihar," *EI²*, Vol. 3, pp. 1246–48.

10. *Al-Mujahid*, 15 December 1993, 15 January, 12 February 1994.

11. Ibid., 3 December 1993; "Qira'at fi Fiqh al-Shahada," pp. 13–15. See also Reuven Paz, *Suicide and Jihad in Palestinian Radical Islam: The Ideological Dimension* (Hebrew; Tel Aviv, August 1998), pp. 13–18.

12. See, e.g., *al-Mujahid Amam al-Tahqiq wal-Ta'dhib* (Nicosia, September 1988), pp. 3–16; *bi-'Inwan Ma'rakat al-Mujahid fi Aqbiyat al-Tahqiq*, pp. 4–7.

13. Shiqaqi's interview in *al-Hayat*, 15 April 1995. See also Sayyid Ahmad, Vol. 2, pp. 1316–19, *al-Mujahid*, 7 November 1997.

14. *Filastin al-Muslima*, May 1996. Tantawi's interview in *al-Hayat*, 12 August; *al-Musawwar* (Cairo), 7 November 1997.

15. Yusuf al-Qirdawi quoted in *Filastin al-Muslima*, September 1996, pp. 50–51; Huwaydi quoted in *al-Ahram*, 5 August 1997. See also Nawaf Ha'il Takruri (ed.), *al-'Amaliyyat al-Istishhadiyya fi al-Mizan al-Fiqhi* (2nd edition, Damascus, 1997). Only minority of the Islamic spectrum held that the perpetrates of suicide acts are not to be considered martyrs. In their view, the phenomenon of suicide missions distorts the image of Islam as a religion of compassion and coexistence, and exposes the defects of the Islamic movements. Spokesmen for this dissident view were Shaykh Nimr Darwish, the spiritual leader of the Islamic movement in Israel, the mufti of Istanbul and the mufti of Saudi Arabia. See *Voice of Palestine* (Jericho), 4, 6 March 1996; *Yedi'ot Aharonot* (Tel Aviv), 29 September 1997; *Ha'aretz* 11 May 2001.

16. See, e.g., *al-Mujahid*, December 1997.

17. Sivan, *Arab Political Myths*, pp. 9–11; Dov Landau, *From Metaphor to Symbol* (Hebrew; Ramat Gan, 1979), pp. 86–91; Ravitzky, pp. 110–12. See also Ram, pp. 6–10.

18. *Al-Mujahid*, 8 June 1990, 20 November 1992; Shiqaqi and Nafi', "al-Qadiyya al-Filastiniyya," p. 12.

19. *Al-Mujahid*, 5 October 1990. See also Kupferschmidt, pp. 253–54.

20. *Al-Mujahid*, 5 October 1990.

21. Ibid.

22. See e.g., *al-Mujahid*, 5 October 1990; *al-Istiqlal*, 21 October 1994, 9 October 1998.

23. *Al-Mujahid*, 4 October 1991.

24. *Ma'ariv*, 11 December 1992.

25. See, e.g., *al-Mujahid*, 5, 22 January 1993; *al-Istiqlal*, 12 January 1996; *Filastin al-Muslima*, December 1994.
26. *Al-Mujahid*, 4 October 1991, 21 May 1993. See also *Shuhadha ma' Sabq al-Israr* (n.p., 1993).
27. Shiqaqi quoted in Sayyid Ahmad, Vol. 2, pp. 1233–35, 1357–61; *al-Mujahid*, 14 June, 1 November 1991; *al-Istiqlal*, 9 February 1994, 10 July 1998.
28. Shiqaqi quoted in Sayyid Ahmad, Vol. 2, p. 1357.
29. *Al-Sha'b*, 30 July 1996; *al-Istiqlal*, 17 July 1998; *al-Mujahid*, 26 October, December 1997. See also *Fathi al-Shiqaqi Shahidan*, pp. 19–20.
30. See, e.g., *al-Mujahid*, 2 March, 26 October 1997; *al-Istiqlal*, 9 October 1998.
31. Sivan, *Arab Political Myths*, p. 131.
32. *Al-Mujahid*, 30 March 1990, 26 February, 19 March 1993.
33. Ibid., 4 May 1990.
34. Ibid., 27 April 1990, 19 March 1993; Shiqaqi quoted in Sayyid Ahmad, Vol. 2, pp. 1383–87.
35. *Al-Mujahid*, 26 January, 24 August 1990; *al-Istiqlal*, 29 October 1998.
36. See also Shaul Mishal and Reuben Aharoni, *Speaking Stones: Communiqués from the Intifada Underground* (New York, 1994), pp. 25–30.
37. See, e.g., *al-Mujahid*, 12 April 1990.

Conclusion

1. Tawfiq al-Tayyib, *al-Khasa'is al-Thabitah al-Lazima wal-Khasa'is al-Muktasiba lil-Haraka al-Islamiyya* (Amman, 1992), pp. 8–14.
2. See, e.g., James P. Piscatori, *Islam in World of Nations-States* (Cambridge, 1986), pp. 40–75.
3. Islamic Jihad charter, p. 9; *Masirat al-Jihad al-Islami fi Filastin*, pp. 7–8.
4. Hamas charter, clause 12.
5. *Ha'aretz*, 2 August 1999; *JP*, 25 December 1999. In July 2000, 'Ali Mustafa replaced Habash as the new general secretary of the PFLP. Mustafa, with the backing of 'Arafat and the consent of Israel, was allowed to return to the territories. This development intensified the dialogue between the PA and the PFLP, although the latter continued to oppose the Oslo Accords. *Ha'aretz*, 9 July 2000.
6. Roy, "Civil Society in the Gaza Strip," pp. 221–26.
7. See, e.g., Robinson, *Building a Palestinian State*, pp. 175–88, 197–200.
8. Shiqaqi, *al-Mashru' al-Islami al-Mu'asir wa-Markaziyyat al-Qadiyya al-Filastiniyya*, pp. 92–94; Islamic Jihad charter, pp. 9–10. See also, *al-Mukhtar al-Islami*, 25 September 1999.
9. Shalah's interviews in *al-Bayadir al-Siyasi*, 14 September 1996, *al-Mukhtar al-Islami*, 25 September 1999. See also Hindi and Shami's interviews in *al-Istiqlal*, 7, 14 August 1998.

10. See, e.g., Nazzal's interview in *al-Hayat*, 4 March 1997; Musa Abu Marzuq quoted in *al-Risala*, 14 October 1999; Salah Shahada's interview in ibid., 18 May 2000.

11. See, e.g., Anat Kurtz and Nahman Tal, *Hamas: Radical Islam in a National Struggle* (Tel Aviv, July 1997), pp. 49–50. For a similar approach see Mishal and Sela, especially pp. 147–51, 163–71.

12. Neil J. Smelser, *Theory of Collective Behavior* (New York, 1963), pp. 120–29, 313–319; Ralph H. Turner and Lewis M. Killian, *Collective Behavior* (2nd edition, New Jersey, 1972), pp. 256–57, 269–74.

13. *Al-Tali'a al-Islamiyya*, August 1983, p. 50; *al-Nur*, August 1980, pp. 3–4; Yusuf al-Qirdawi, *al-Sabr fi al-Qur'an* (Cairo, 1970), p. 12.

14. Hamid Bitawi, *Khutab Da'iya* (Nablus, 1992) 2 vols.; Bitawi's interview in *al-Istiqlal*, 17 July 1998; the Salvation Party's platform (Gaza, 1996); *al-Risala*, 17 June 1999, p. 15. See also the platform of the Islamic Resistance Movement (*Harakat al-Nidal al-Islami*) in *Ara' Fikriyya wa-Mawaqif Siyasiyya* (Gaza, n.d.), especially pp. 29–46.

15. See, e.g., *Ha'aretz*, 8 May 1998; *al-Risala*, 1 July, 21, 28 October 1999. An important forum for the 'ulama's views on social matters was provided by *al-Bayan*, an Islamic journal sponsored by the PA.

16. 'Akrama Sabri quoted in *al-Risala*, 1 July 1999.

17. Hamas leaflet, 16 September 1996.

18. *The Palestinian NGO Project* (n.p., April 1997), pp. 1–3. See also Hasan Lidadawa, "al-Sulta al-Wataniyya al-Filastiniyya wal-Munazzamat Ghair al-Hukumiyya," *al-Siyasa al-Filastiniyya* (Summer 1999), pp. 127–43. On informal civil networks and political dissent see Guilain Denoeux, *Urban Unrest in the Middle East* (Albany, New York, 1993), especially pp. 21–26, 193–211.

19. Shiqaqi, "Didda al-Sharq al-Awsat al-Jadid," pp. 569–72. See also Islamic Jihad charter, pp. 3, 5, 10.

20. Shiqaqi's interviews in *Kayhan al-'Arabi*, 21 August 1993; *al-Wasat*, 30 January 1995; Shiqaqi, "Didda al-Sharq al-Awsat al-Jadid," pp. 569–72; Shalah quoted in *al-Mujahid*, December 1997; 'Azzam quoted in *al-Istiqlal*, 9 October 1998. See also Ibrahim Ghawsha's interview in *al-'Alam*, 9 October 1993.

21. Fadlallah's interviews in *al-'Alam*, 16 October; *Filastin al-Muslima*, November 1993.

22. See, e.g., *al-Istiqlal*, 5, 26 October 2000; Musa Abu Marzuq's interview in *Filastin al-Muslima*, October 2000; ibid., November 2000; *Middle East International*, 8 December 2000, pp. 7–8.

23. *Al-Istiqlal*, 26 October 2000.

24. See, e.g., Ahmad Yasin's interview in *Filastin al-Muslima*, November 2000.

25. Shalah's interview in *al-Istiqlal*, 5 October 2000.

Appendix: The Islamic Jihad's Internal Charter
(selected segments)

Name and Definition

The Islamic Jihad is a fighting movement that upholds Islam as a religion and a state and serves as the vanguard of the revolutionary Islamic movement. Its leader is Dr. Fathi al-Shiqaqi, who bases himself on the *shura* and functions through the recognized bodies.

The Features of the Movement

1. Religious: Its aims, principles and activities derive from the glorious Islamic heritage.
2. Combatant: It upholds the scared jihad as the only solution for the liberation of Palestine and the destruction of the heretical regimes.
3. Comprehensive: It perceives Islam as a comprehensive framework not subject to division or annulment.
4. Unifying: It believes in Islamic unity, based on justice, equality and fraternity.
5. Vanguard: It leads the Arab and Muslim peoples and mobilizes them to defend their identity.
6. Worldwide: It perceives the universe as Islamic territory which must be liberated from heresy.
7. Benevolent: It aims to restore the dignity of the Muslim, which has been crushed by the West and by Zionism.
8. Ethical: It oversees private and public morality, as commanded by Islam.
9. Military: It enhances military activity and reveals its true meaning.
10. Consultant: It regards the *shura* as the authentic and firm source for decision-making.
11. Independent: It is not subordinate to any internal or external force.
12. Uniqueness: It is a unique phenomenon among the Islamic movements with a specific platform.

Ideological Guidelines

1. Adherence to the Islamic faith as represented by the first generation of righteous Muslims and the pure companions of the Prophet.
2. Combining tradition and modernity and taking from them those elements that do not contradict Islam.

---

3. Cleaving to jihad and eschewing the path of gradual reform.
4. Promoting Islamic unity with the fighting Islamic forces, while preserving organizational independence.
5. Eschewing ideological tyranny or juridical exclusivism.
6. Distrust of the 'ulama', who are servants of tyranny.
7. Forbidding confrontation and killing between Muslims.
8. Positing the masses as the vehicle of the revolution and its strategic depth in the face of oppressors.
9. Forbidding any ideological convergence between heresy and faith, or between exponents of secularism and the movement.
10. Conducting movement policy and activity in accordance with the viewpoint of Islam.
11. Palestine is part of the faith. To relinquish any part of it is to abandon Islam.

Basic Themes

1. The Palestinian problem is the central issue of the modern Islamic movement and represents the focus of the existential struggle today.
2. The struggle is comprehensive, directed at the triple heresy and oppression of the West, the Arab regimes and Israel.
3. Islamization of the struggle against the Zionist enemy, alongside rejecting national and patriotic perceptions, which seek to marginalize the struggle.
4. Rejecting the political solution to the Palestinian problem and sanctifying jihad and martyrdom as the only means for liberating the land.
5. Perceiving the Islamic movement in the world as the sole spokesman of the people and the authentic alternative to the heretic regimes.
6. The Arab regimes and Israel are two sides of the same coin. They are the product of Western aggression against the Muslim world.
7. Avoiding conflict with Palestinian national forces and restoring the unity of the Palestinian people.
8. Prohibiting entry into PLO institutions so long as that organization does not truly adopt the Islamic option.
9. Boycotting the parliamentary bodies of the heretical states or the forming of alliances with them.
10. Perceiving the separatist and Westernized regimes as apostates that must be eliminated.
11. Promoting cooperation with non-Islamic fighting forces against the common enemy.
12. Supporting oppressed peoples and movements in the world against the forces of imperialism.

General and Specific Goals

The ultimate goal is satisfying Allah; the earthly goal is to promote the revival of Islam.

The general goals: 1. Imbuing the Palestinian character with a binding Islamic imprint. 2. Advancing popular revolution. 3. Realizing Islamic unity through jihad. 4. Liberating the sacred land from the Zionist occupation. 5. Establishing Islamic rule over the land from which the Prophet ascended to heaven.

The specific goals: 1. Sapping the enemy forces and eroding its material and economic resources. 2. Spreading fear and anxiety among the Zionists, and especially the settlers, so as to force them to abandon their homes. 3. Creating an emotional barrier between the Jews and the Muslim Palestinian people and combating advocates of Arab-Israeli coexistence. 4. Terminating economic and financial dependence on the enemy. 5. Obstructing the peace agreements between the treacherous Arab regimes and the Zionist entity.

Slogans

1. Islam is the only solution to the struggle.
2. Neither East nor West, only Islam.
3. Jihad is the way of liberation.
4. Our struggle is for existence and not for boundaries.
5. Jihad is the way to unity, and unity is the way to strength and power.
6. Martyrdom gives vitality to life.
7. No movement has any existence without a public.
8. There is no peace without Islam.
9. The Muslim peoples are the strategic depth of the Intifada.
10. The Intifada belongs to the people and must not be relinquished.
11. There is no place for treason and no mercy for those who cooperate with the enemy.
12. Patience is faith and despair is heresy.
13. Understanding the real nature of the enemy will contribute to the liberation of the land.
14. The dowry of freedom is blood.
15. Victory or martyrdom are the way of jihad.

Organizational Principles

1. Belief in the unity of the fighting Islamic movement.
2. Loyalty to Islam and to the movement platform.

3. Obedience to the movement leadership.
4. Dedication and self-sacrifice without arrogance.
5. Balance between the conceptual and the organizational.
6. Self-criticism as the path to organizational purity.

Means

Means and modus operandi change and evolve according to the circumstances of the time. The important means include:

1. Conducting guerrilla warfare (attacking and escaping).
2. Using popular revolutionary means and imbuing the resistance with a broader character.
3. Purifying society from spies, who are not entitled to repent, and rehabilitating the deviants who did not display close links to the enemy.
4. Heightening the security awareness of the public so as not to be trapped by the enemy.
5. Emphasizing the misery of the Palestinian people through using every possible forum.
6. Using technological means.
7. Disseminating the movement's ideas by the use of every available channel, especially mosques, schools and campuses.

The Membership Base of the Movement

The movement views every Muslim living in Palestine or dedicating his time and energy to liberating Palestine as its natural depth everywhere.

The Movement's Identity

The movement is Palestinian in its character and Islamic in its essence. It places Palestine as the focus of the struggle and Islam as its ideology.

Non-Muslims in Palestine

The Christians are protected subjects (*dhimmis*). They have the same rights as Muslims, which must not be violated except in cases of allegiance to the enemy and its allies.

The Non-Islamic Movements

Dialogue and freedom of opinion are a sacred right, on condition that they do not harm the faith and heritage of the Muslim nation. All internal bloodshed is forbidden, as force must be directed solely against the enemy. Cooperation and tactical alliances must be promoted with movements and parties that reject the peace process in the region.

The Islamic Movements

The position toward the Islamic movements should be based on Allah's words, "Believers are brothers." One must not enter into conflict or struggle with them and must treat them with respect so long as this does not lead to serious damage or corruption.

The Arab Regimes

The Arab regimes are heretical and tyrannical, and should not be cooperated with or assisted. Their impotence should be exposed by all legitimate means so as to overthrow them.

The Peace Process

A solution of peace based on the recognition of the Jews' right in Palestine, or part of it, contradicts the Qur'an, since this means relinquishing Islamic holy land. All international and Arab conferences which promote this solution are deceivers, serving only the enemy. The struggle will be carried on until the universal role of Islam is realized once more.

The Struggle in Palestine

The struggle between Islam and the West is a cultural one, embodied in the Zionist presence in Palestine. This struggle must be viewed from the Qur'anic perspective, which points to the inevitability of the Jews gathering in Palestine and to Zionist corruption, but also assures the final victory of Islam.

Patriotism and Nationalism

There is no contradiction between patriotism and nationalism, and Islam, if the meaning of patriotism is love of the land and defending its territories and sanctities; and if the meaning of nationalism is love of the people, saving them from oppressors and defending their rights. These concepts are an integral part of the greater message—Islam. However, if the meaning is loyalty to land instead of glorifying Islam, then this is heresy which must be combatted.

Communal Activity

Communal activity is based on moral and pragmatic foundations distant from the abstract concept or the rigid idea. It comprises religious and military activity simultaneously, with the personality of the believer molded through involvement in the struggle and sacrificing his soul for Islam.

The Regimes in Muslim Countries

The fate of these regimes is the same as that of the Arab regimes, products of imperialism and an expression of separatism and Westernization. An exception is the Islamic regime in Iran, which is considered to be the strategic depth of the Islamic revolution in the region.

The Double-edged Struggle in Palestine

The Palestinians are the people of the sacred land. They are the warhead against the Zionist entity. The destruction of the treacherous Arab regimes is part of the destruction of the Zionist entity, since these regimes constitute the fence surrounding this entity. It is impossible to separate jihad against the infidel regimes from jihad against the Khaybarite entity.* The jihad platform must be implemented seriously and comprehensively.

The Woman

The woman is the primary educational institution for raising and preparing heroes to carry on the struggle against the occupation and heresy. For this she must receive an education and guidance. She constitutes a substantive and integral factor in the liberation campaign and must be allowed to take part in the political and military fight against the enemy.

---

* Khaybar was a rich, fertile oasis in Hijaz inhabited by Jews. It was conquered by the Muslims, led by the Prophet, in 628.

The New World Order

The new world order, which was crystallized after the collapse of Communism and was led by the US and the West, is a graver enemy than the previous order. It constitutes a great danger to Islam and to Muslims, primarily after it declared war against the Islamic trend throughout the world.

Entering Parliamentry bodies

This strategy is rejected and deviates from rightful Islamic teachings. It constitutes a kind of truce with the infidel [Arab] regimes and grants legitimation to their existence.

Civic Participation

This issue is dependent on local circumstances. Entry into public bodies is permissible if this serves Islam, Muslims and the Islamic movement. However, one should not rely on them overly or view them as the sole means to promote change in society.

The Priorities of the Movement

The priorities of the movement are focused on the occupied land. The leading priority is military activity to sap the enemy and demoralize its ranks. Then comes civil activity in various areas according to the resources and capabilities at the disposal of the movement.

The Accusation of Heresy (Takfir)

The movement perceives Arab societies, including the Palestinian one, as paralyzed Islamic societies which must be transformed from a state of passivity to a state of revolution against the tyranny of the Israeli occupation and of the corrupted [Arab] regimes. An accusation of heresy is never collective, but relates to a specific individual or party who consciously and deliberately has deviated from Islam in views or conduct.

International Forums (as the UN)

These bodies are mere devices to advance the intrigues and crimes of the great Satan, the US. They legitimize evil and cancel out justice. They are imperialistic organizations that use every means to destroy Islam and to fight against the oppressed. Hence, all of their decisions are null and void. One should not rely on them or be assisted by them. Nevertheless, since these forums serve as an international platform, it is permissible to join them in order to create a new balance of power with the West and break its dominance in decision-making.

The Arab League

This forum reflects the state of separatism, divisiveness and dispute in the Arab world. The League represents Arab defeatism and is the creation of imperialism. One should not trust it or rely on it. Nevertheless, taking part in it is permissible in order to turn it into a lever for improving the Arab reality.

Bibliography

Newspapers and Periodicals

Al-'Ahd (Beirut)
Al-'Alam (London)
Al-Anba (Kuwait)
Al-Ayyam (Ramallah, West Bank).
Al-Bayan (Gaza)
Al-Bilad (Amman)
Al-Dustur (Amman)
Ettela'at (Tehran)
Al-Fajr (East Jerusalem)
Filustin al-Muslima (London)
Filastin al-Thawra (Nicosia)
Foreign Report (London)
Ha'aretz (Tel Aviv)
Al-Hayat (London)
Al-Hayat al-Jadida (Gaza)
Al-Hilal al-Duwali (Tehran)
Al-Islam wa-Filastin (Nicosia)
Al-Istiqlal (Gaza)
Jerusalem Report (Jerusalem)
Kayhan al-'Arabi (Tehran)
Kayhan International (Tehran)
Al-Khalij (Abu Dhabi)
Al-Liwa (Amman)
Ma'ariv (Tel Aviv)
Al-Majalla (London)
Majallat al-Dirasat al-Filastiniyya (Beirut)
Al-Majd (Amman)
Al-Mujahid (Beirut)
Al-Mujahid (Gaza)
Al-Mujtama' (Kuwait)
Al-Mukhtar al-Islami (Cairo)
Al-Nur (East Jerusalem)
Al-Qabas (Kuwait)
Al-Quds (East Jerusalem)
Al-Risala (Gaza)
Al-Sabil (Oslo)
Al-Sharq al-Awsat (London)
Al-Shira' (Beirut)
Shu'un Filastiniyya (Nicosia)
Al-Siyasa al-Filastiniyya (Nablus)
Al-Tali'a al-Islamiyya (London)

Tariq al-Intisar (Nicosia)
Al-Wahda (Beirut)
Al-Wasat (London)
Al-Watan al-'Arabi (London)

Leaflets

Islamic Jihad's leaflets from *al-Islam wa-Filastin* (1988–1990), *al-Mujahid* (1990–1997)

Books and Articles

Abu 'Amr, Ziad. *Islamic Fundamentalism in the West Bank and Gaza Strip*. Indiana, 1994.
Ahmad, Hisham H. *Hamas From Religious Salvation to Political Transformation*. Jerusalem, 1994.
Ajami, Fouad. *The Arab Predicament*. Cambridge, 1981.
Al-'Alami, Sa'd al-Din. *Watha'iq al-Hayha al-Islamiyya al-'Ulya 1967–1984*. Jerusalem, 1984.
Altman, Israel. "Islamic Movements in Egypt," *The Jerusalem Quarterly*, Vol. 10 (Winter 1979), pp. 87–105.
Ayalon, Ami. *Language and Change in the Arab Middle East*. New York, 1987.
Al-Barghuthi, Iyyad. *al-Haraka al-Islamiyya al-Filastiniyya wal-Nizam al-'Alami al-Jadid*. Jerusalem, 1992.
Barkun, Michael. *Disaster and Millenium*. New Haven, 1974.
Bengio, Ofra. *Saddam's Word: Political Discourse in Iraq*. Oxford, 1998.
Bin Yusuf, Ahmad (ed.). *Hamas Hadath 'Abir am Badil Da'im*. n.p., 1990.
Bitawi, Hamid. *Khutab Da'iya*. Nablus, 1992. 2 Vol.
Cassirer, Ernest. *Language and Myth*. New York, 1946.
Cobban, Helena. "The PLO and the Intifada," *MEJ*, Vol. 44, No. 2 (Spring 1990), pp. 207–33.
Cohen, Amnon. *Political Parties in the West Bank Under the Jordanian Regime 1949–1967*. London, 1982.
Cohen, Shalom. "Khomeinism in Gaza," *New Outlook* (March 1980), pp. 6–9.
Denoeux, Guilain. *Urban Unrest in the Middle East*. Albany, 1993.
Dessouki, Ali E. "The Islamic Resurgence, Sources, Dynamics and Implications," in idem (ed.). *Islamic Resurgence in the Arab World*. New York, 1982, pp. 3–9.
Eisenstadt, S.N (ed.). *Max Weber on Charisma and Institution Building*. Chicago, 1968.
Fadlallah, Muhammad Husayn. "Ab'ad Ittifaq Ghazza-Ariha fi al-Waqi' al-Filastini wal-'Arabi," *Qira'at Siyasiyya*, Vol. 4 (Winter 1994), pp. 85–94.
Faraj, 'Abd al-Salam. *al-Farida al-Gha'iba*. Cairo, 1982.
Fasheh, Munir. "Political Islam in the West Bank," *Merip Reports*, No. 103 (February 1982), p. 16.
Ganor, Boaz. "Islamic Jihad," *Matara*, No. 19 (1991), pp. 24–36.
Gellner, Ernest. *Conditions of Liberty: Civil Society and its Rivals*. New York, 1994.

Al-Ghazali, Muhammad. *Min Huna Na'lamu*. 5th edition, Cairo, n.p.

Al-Harub, Khalid. "Harakat Hamas wal-Ta'ddudiḍyya al-Diniyya wal-Siyasiyya," in Jawad Ahmad and Iyyad al-Barghuthi (eds.). *Dirasa fi al-Fikr al-Siyasi li-Hamas*. Amman, 1997, pp. 173–83.

Hatina, Meir. "Iran and the Palestinian Islamic Movement," *Orient* 38, No. 1 (1997), pp. 107–20.

——. "Egypt," *MECS*, Vol. XXI (1997), pp. 301–40.

——. "Hamas and the Oslo Accords: Religious Dogma in a Changing Political Reality," *Mediterranean Politics*, Vol. 4, No. 3 (Autumn 1999), pp. 37–55

Hawwa, Sa'id. *al-Khumayniyya Shudhudh fi al-'Aqa'id wa Shudhudh fi al-Mawaqif*. Cairo, 1987.

Al-Hufash, 'Umar and 'Awad, Khalid. *Mub'adu Marj al-Zuhur*. Jerusalem, 1994.

Ibn Qasim, 'Abd al-Rahman. *Majmu' Fatawat Shaykh al-Islam Ahmad Ibn Taymiyya*. Cairo, n.p., Vol. 3.

Ibrahim, Saad Eddin. "Anatomy of Egypt's Islamic Groups: Methodological Note and Preliminary Findings," *IJMES*, Vol. 12 (1980), pp. 423–53.

'Isa, 'Abdallah. *Hafilat al-Jihad al-Islami*. Amman, 1991.

Israeli Civil Administration. *Information Data: The West Bank and Gaza Strip*. Hebrew; n.p, November–December 1983.

——. *The Gaza Strip: Political Profile*. n.p., April 1986.

——. *The Islamic Activity in the West Bank*. n.p. April 1988.

Al-Jarbawi, 'Ali. *al-Intifada wal-Qiyadat al-Siyasiyya fi al-Daffa al-Gharbiyya wa-Qita Ghazza*. Beirut, 1989.

——."Mawqif al-Harakat al-Islamiyya min al-Ittifaq al-Filastini al-Isra'ili," *al-Mustaqbal al-'Arabi* (February 1994), pp. 57–58.

Jubran, Michel and Drake, Laura. "The Islamist Fundamentalist Movement in the West Bank and Gaza Strip," *Middle East Policy*, Vol. 2, No. 2 (1993), pp. 1–15.

Khadduri, Majid. *War and Peace in the Law of Islam*. Baltimore, 1955.

Klein, Menachem. "Competing Brothers: The Web of Hamas-PLO Relations," in Bruce Maddy-Weitzman and Efraim Inbar (eds.). *Religious Radicalism in the Greater Middle East*. London, 1997, pp. 111–32.

Kramer, Martin. "Redeeming Jerusalem: The Pan-Islamic Premise of Hizballah," in David Menashri (ed.). *The Iranian Revolution and the Muslim World*. Boulder, 1990, pp. 106–26.

——. "Concluding Chapter: The Renewal Shi'a," in idem. *Protest and Revolution in Shi'i Islam* (Hebrew; Tel Aviv, 1986), pp. 141–54.

——. "Sacrifice and 'Self-Martyrdom' in Shi'ite Lebanon," in idem. *Arab Awakening and Islamic Revival*. New Brunswick, 1996, pp. 231–43.

Kupferschmidt, Uri M. *The Supreme Muslim Council: Islam under the British Mandate for Palestine*. Leiden, 1987.

Kurtz, Anat and Tal Nahman. *Hamas: Radical Islam in a National Struggle*. Tel Aviv, July 1997.

Landau, Dov. *From Metaphor to Symbol*. Hebrew; Ramat Gan, 1979.

Lazarus-Yafeh, Hava. "Contemporary Fundamentalism, Judaism, Christianity, Islam," *The Jerusalem Quarterly*, No. 47 (Summer 1988), pp. 27–39.

Legrain, Jean Francois. "The Islamic Movement and the Intifada," in Jamal R. Nassar and Roger Heacock (eds.). *Intifada: Palestine at the Crossroads*. New York, 1990, pp. 176–81.

Lidadawa, Hasan. "al-Sulta al-Wataniyya al-Filastiniyya wal-Munazzamat Ghair al-Hukumiyya," *al-Siyasa al-Filastiniyya* (Summer 1999), pp. 127–43.

Litvak, Meir. *Islam and Democracy in the Arab World.* Hebrew; Tel Aviv, 1998.

——. "The Islamization of the Palestinian-Israeli Conflict: The Case of Hamas," *MES*, Vol. 34, No. 1 (January 1998), pp. 148–63.

Al-Madhun, Rab'i. "al-Haraka al-Islamiyya fi Filastin," *Shu'un Filastiniyya*, No. 187 (October 1988), pp. 10–50.

Mayer, Thomas. "Pro-Iranian Fundamentalism in Gaza," in Emmanuel Sivan and Menachem Friedman (eds.). *Religious Radicalism and Politics in the Middle East.* Albany, 1990, pp. 143–55.

Menashri, David. *Iran: A Decade of War and Revolution.* New York, 1990.

——. "Iran," *MECS*, Vol. XXI (1997), pp. 341–71.

Milton-Edwards, Beverley. *Islamic Politics in Palestine.* London, 1996.

Mishal, Shaul and Aharoni, Reuben. *Speaking Stones: Communiqués from the Intifada Underground.* New York, 1994.

Mishal, Shaul and Sela, Avraham. *The Palestinian Hamas: Visions, Violence, and Coexistence.* New York, 1999.

Muru, Muhammad, *Fathi al-Shiqaqi.* Cairo, 1997.

Muslih, Muhammad. "Palestinian Civil Society," in Norton (ed.). *Civil Society in the Middle East.* Leidin, 1995, Vol. 1, pp. 243–68.

Mustafa, Hala. "al-Tayyar al-Islami fi al-Ard al-Muhtalah," *al-Mustaqbal al-'Arabi*, July 1988, pp. 75–90.

Al-Nabhani, Taqi al-Din. *Nizam al-Islam.* 2nd edition, Jerusalem, 1953.

Al-Nasir, Husam. *Hamas al-Intilaq wa-Mu'adalat al-Sira'.* n.p., n.d.

Norton, Augustus R. "Introduction," in idem. *Civil Society in the Middle East*, Vol. 1. pp. 1–25.

Paz, Reuven [M.A degree]. *The Development of the Palestinian Islamic Factors between 1967–1988.* Hebrew; Haifa, 1989.

——. *Suicide and Jihad in Palestinian Radical Islam: The Ideological Dimension.* Hebrew; Tel Aviv, 1998.

Peters, Rudolph. *Islam and Colonialism.* The Hague, 1979.

Pipes, Daniel. *In the Path of God: Islam and Political Power.* New York, 1983.

Piscatori, James P. *Islam in World of Nations-States.* Cambridge, 1986.

Al-Qirdawi, Yusuf. *al-Sabr fi al-Qur'an.* Cairo, 1970.

Qutb, Sayyid. *Ma'alim fi al-Tariq.* Cairo, n.p.

Ram, Haggay. *Myth and Mobilization in Revolutionary Iran.* Washington D.C., 1994.

Ravitzky, Aviezer. *Freedom Inscribed.* Hebrew; Tel Aviv, 1999.

Rekhess, Elie. "The Iranian Impact on the Islamic Jihad Movement in the Gaza Strip," in David Menashri (ed.). *The Iranian Revolution and the Muslim World*, pp. 189–206.

Rekhess, Elie and Meir Litvak. "Palestinian Affairs," *MECS*, Vol. XIX (1995), pp. 135–68.

——. "Palestinian Affairs," *MECS*, Vol. XX (1996), pp. 138–66.

Robinson, Glenn E. *Building a Palestinian State.* Bloomington, 1997.

Rosenthal, Franz. "Intihar," EI^2, Vol. 3, pp. 1246–48.

Roy, Sara. "Civil Society in the Gaza Strip: Obstacles to Social Reconstruction," in Norton (ed.). *Civil Society in the Middle East*, Vol. 2, pp. 221–58.

Sahliyeh, Emile. *In Search of Leadership: West Bank Politics Since 1967.* Washington D.C., 1988.

Sarbal, Ibrahim. *Harakat al-Jihad al-Islami Kata'ib al-Aqsa*. Amman, 1990.

Satloff, Robert. "Islam in the Palestinian Uprising," *Orbis*, No. 33 (Summer 1989), pp. 389–401.

Sayyid Ahmad, Rif'at (ed.). *Rihlat al-Damm alladhi Hazama al-Sayf*. Cairo, 1996, 2 vols.

Schiff, Ze'ev and Ya'ari, Ehud. *Intifada*. New York, 1989.

Schoch, Bernd. *The Islamic Movement: A Challenge for Palestinian State-Building*. Jerusalem, 1999.

Shadid, Muhammad K. "The Muslim Brotherhood Movement in the West Bank and Gaza," *Third World Quarterly* (April 1988), pp. 658–62.

Shepard, William E. "Islam and Ideology: Towards a Typology," *IJMES*, Vol. 19, No. 3 (August 1987), pp. 307–36.

Al-Shiqaqi, Fathi. *al-Khumayni al-Hall al-Islami wal-Badil*. Cairo, 1979.

——. *al-Mashru' al-Islami al-Mu'asir fi Filastin*. n.p., 1995.

——. *al-Mashru' al-Islami al-Mu'asir wa-Markaziyyat al-Qadiyya al-Filastiniyya*. n.p., December 1988.

——. *al-Istiqlal wal-Tab'iyya al-Hawd al-'Arabi al-Islami*. n.p., n.d.

Sivan, Emmanuel. *Radical Islam*. New Haven, 1985.

——. *Arab Political Myths*. Hebrew; Tel Aviv, 1988.

——. "Radical Islam—Comparative Aspects," in *Radical Islam: Hamas and the PLO at the Crossroad* (Hebrew; Jerusalem, February 1993), pp. 1–9.

Smelser, Neil J. *Theory of Collective Behavior*. New York, 1963.

Smith, Donald E. *Religion and Political Development*. Boston, 1970.

Steinberg, Matti. "The PLO and Palestinian Islamic Fundamentalism," *The Jerusalem Quarterly*, No. 52 (Fall 1989), pp. 37–54.

Strindberg, Anders. "The Damascus-Based Alliance of Palestinian Forces: A Primer," *Journal of Palestinian Studies*, Vol. 29, No. 3 (Spring 2000), pp. 60–76.

Taji-Farouki, Suha. "Islamists and the Threat of Jihad: Hizb al-Tahrir and the al-Muhajiroun on Israel and the Jews," *MES*, Vol. 36, No. 4 (October 2000), pp.21–46.

Takruri, Nawaf Ha'il (ed.). *Al-'Amaliyyat al-Istishhadiyya fi al-Mizan al-Fiqhi*. 2nd edition., Damascus, 1997.

Al-Tayyib, Tawfiq. *al-Hall al-Islami ma ba'd al-Nakbatayn*. 3rd edition, Cairo, 1985.

——. *al-Khasa'is al-Thabitah al-Lazima wal-Khasa'is al-Muktasiba lil-Haraka al-Islamiyya*. Amman, 1992.

Teitelbaum, Joshua. "The Palestinian Liberation Organization," *MECS*, Vol. XII (1988), pp. 229–76.

Thabit, Muhsin. *Nashat al-Jama'a al-Islamiyya fi Sujun al-Ihtilal al-Israi'li*. n.p., n.d.

Thrupp, Sylvia L. (ed.). *Millennial Dreams in Action*. New York, 1970.

Turner, Ralp H. and Killian, Lewis M. *Collective Behavior*. 2nd edition, New Jersey, 1972.

Yasin, 'Abd al-Qadir. "Mawqi' Hamas fi al-Zahira al-Islamiyya fi al-Daffa wal-Qita'," *al-Urdunn al-Jadid* (Autumn 1988), pp. 43–53.

Zakariyya, Muhammad. "al-Intifada wal-Islah al-Tanzimi fi Munazzamat al-Tahrir al-Filastini," *al-Fikr al-Dimuqrati*, Vol. 5 (Winter 1988), pp. 22–31.

Zamel, Abdulaziz I. [M.A degree]. *The Rise of Palestinian Islamist Groups*. Tampa, 1991.

Zebiri, Kate. *Mahmud Shaltut and Islamic Modernism*. Oxford, 1993.

Unattributed books and essays

Afkar Siyasiyya li-Hizb al-Tahrir. Beirut, 1994.
Bi-'Inwan Ma'rakat al-Mujahid fi Aqbiyat al-Tahqiq. n.p., n.d.
Al-Dimuqratiyya Da'ia. Gaza, 1994.
Fathi al-Shiqaqi Shahidan. Beirut, 1996.
Fi Sabil Jabha Islamiyya Mutahidah. n.p., n.d.
Filastin Qadiyya Islamiyya. n.p., n.d.
Filastin wal-Intifada. Chicago, April 1988.
Harakat al-Jihad al-Islami Bayt al-Maqdis. Amman, 1991.
Harakat al-Nidal al-Islami fi Filastin, Ara' Fikriyya wa-Mawaqif Siyasiyya. Gaza, n.d.
Hiwar ma' Ahmad Jibril: al-Thawra wal-Mutaghayyirat al-Dawliyya. Damascus, 1990.
Al-Islam Tariq al-Intisar. Chicago, June 1991.
Al-La'iha al-Dakhiliyya (Islamic Jihad's internal charter). n.p., n.d.
Masirat al-Jihad-al-Islami fi Filastin. Beirut, 1989.
Mithaq Harakat al-Muqawama al-Islamiyya—Filastin (Hamas). n.p., 1988.
Al-Mujahid amam al-Tahqiq wal-Ta'dhib. Nicosia, September 1988.
"Qira'at fi Fiqh al-Shahada," *al-Islam wa-Filastin*, 5 June 1988, pp. 3–15.
Al-Sabil fi Muraqabat al-Nafs wal-Tashih. n.p., n.d.
Shuhadha ma' Sabq al-Israr. n.p., 1993.
The Palestinian NGO Project. n.p., April 1997.

Index